THE EVIDENCE OF
THINGS UNSEEN

*Faith Revealed in a Family, in a
Community and a Nation*

JERRY AVETA

WESTBOW
PRESS®
A DIVISION OF THOMAS NELSON
& ZONDERVAN

WestBow Press books may be ordered through booksellers or by contacting:

WestBow Press
A Division of Thomas Nelson & Zondervan
1663 Liberty Drive
Bloomington, IN 47403
www.westbowpress.com
844-714-3454

ISBN: 978-1-6642-4698-0 (sc)
ISBN: 978-1-6642-4699-7 (hc)
ISBN: 978-1-6642-4697-3 (e)

Library of Congress Control Number: 2021920703

Print information available on the last page.

WestBow Press rev. date: 10/23/2021

CONTENTS

PART 4: FAITH FOR THE TIMES

DEDICATION

There is no doubt in my mind that my father had great influence on the shaping of the man that I am and the direction of my life as it has happened. He was not a verbal man, not one to engage in philosophical discussions at least not with me. He modeled what he valued through hard work, determination, dedication, and love of his family. He died a relatively young man, before I could realize the impact that he had made on my life and long before I had a chance to thank him for it. He also died much too soon for me to ask him the thousand questions I now have about him as a man and his life. I know nothing about his war experience because he never mentioned a word about it even when he would watch those simulated war programs on tv. I now wonder what he thought as he watched them. I tried to investigate his military records but by some fluke they were all destroyed in a warehouse fire in St. Louis many years ago. I did manage to have a few of the blanks of his life filled in by his baby sister, my 90-year-old aunt before she recently passed. So, in response to all this I would like to dedicate this writing to my father. It is the only means at my disposal that I have to say "Thanks, Dad, for your investment in me, our family, and this country. Love you."

EPIGRAPH

ABRAHAM LNCOLN'S
SECOND INAUGURAL ADDRESS

Fellow countrymen:

At this second appearing to take the oath of the presidential office, there is less occasion for an extended address than there was at the first. Then a statement, somewhat in detail, of a course to be pursued, seemed fitting and proper. Now, at the expiration of four years, during which public declarations have been constantly called forth on every point and phase of the great contest which stills absorbs the attention, and engrosses the energies of the nation, little that is new could be presented. The progress of our arms, upon which all else chiefly depends, is as well known to the public as myself; and it is, I trust, reasonably satisfactory and encouraging to all. With high hope for the future, no prediction in regard to it is ventured.

On the occasion corresponding to this four years ago, all thoughts were anxiously directed to an impending civil-war. All dreaded it – all sought to avert it. While the inaugural address was being delivered from this place, devoted altogether to *saving* the Union without war, insurgent agents were in the city seeking to *destroy* it without war – seeking to dissolve the Union, and divide the effects, by negotiation. <u>Both parties deprecated war, but one of them would *make* war rather than let the nation survive; and the other would *accept* war rather than let it perish. And the war came.</u>

One eighth of the population were colored slaves, not distributed generally over the Union, but localized in the Southern part of it. These slaves constituted a peculiar and powerful interest. All knew that this interest was, somehow, the cause of the war. To strengthen, perpetuate, and extend the interest was the object of which the insurgents would rend the Union, even by war; while the government claimed no right to do more than to restrict the territorial enlargement of it. Neither party expected for the war, the magnitude, or the duration, which it has already attained. Neither anticipated that the *cause* of the conflict might cease with, or even before, the conflict itself should cease. Each looked for an easier triumph, and a result less fundamental and astounding. <u>Both read the same Bible, and pray to the same God; and each invokes His aid against the other. It may seem strange that any men should dare to ask a just God's assistance in wringing their bread from the sweat of other men's faces; but let us judge not lest we be judged. The prayers of both could not be answered; that of neither has been answered fully. The Almighty has His own purposes.</u> "Woe unto the world because of offenses! For it must needs be that offenses come; but woe to that man by whom the offence cometh!" If we shall suppose that American Slavery is one of those offences which, in the providence of God, must needs come, but which, having continued through His appointed time, He now wills to remove, and that He gives to both North and South, this terrible war, as the woe due to those who by whom the offence came, shall we discern therein any departure from those divine attributes which the believers in a Living God always ascribe to Him? Fondly do we hope – fervently do we pray – that this mighty scourge of war may speedily pass away. <u>Yet, if God wills that it continue, until all</u>

the wealth piled by the bond-man's two hundred and fifty years of unrequited toil shall be sunk, and until every drop of blood drawn with the lash, shall be paid by another drawn with the sword, as was said three thousand years ago, so still it must be said "the judgements of the Lord, are true and righteous altogether."

With malice toward none; with charity for all; with firmness in the right, as God gives us to see the right, let us strive on to finish the work we are in; to bind up the nation's wounds; to care for him who shall have born the battle, and for his widow, and his orphan – to do all which may achieve and cherish a just, and a lasting peace, among ourselves, and with all nations.

Note: Underlined portions referenced in Chapter 12 of text.

PREFACE

I lived on the eastern shore of Virginia in close proximity to the ocean for several years. It was a routine experience when walking on the beach to find ocean debris washed up on the shoreline. If you took the time to closely examine those items scattered throughout the sand you could find evidence of various aspects of plant, animal, and human life. Driftwood, an occasional sandal or sneaker and an unlimited number of shells of all colors, shapes, and sizes are evidence of life that has been lived in some shape or form in and around the ocean. If you have spent any time on the beach, you would know that finding a conch shell was a rare find. Once in a while you may be lucky enough to step on one while in the ocean, but very seldom do you find one on shore. One day walking on the beach after a snowfall I came across dozens of conch shells, some slightly buried under the snow. There were too many to gather, so I focused only on the best-preserved shells to collect. Even after my selection of only the best shells, there were still more than I could carry even after several trips back to my car. Each time I uncovered another conch shell from under the snow it was a thrill and an experience I will never forget.

Writing this text has been like that conch shell experience for me. What started out as a journaling process matured to an effort to create a coherent message of faith relevant to our current times. In so doing I rediscovered the pleasure of sharing views, experiences and thoughts that were hidden under the cold snows of my heart as I began to write. The joy of communicating about God and what He has done in my life fueled my 30 years of ministry. That joy was restored to my life with the creation of this book. In it I hope to provide a message that leverages my experiences in the faith to help project a path forward to future faith generations. That experience for me at this stage of my life I feel is as rare as that conch shell find.

My intent with this writing is to provoke thought in the evangelical community of faith to perhaps be open to some fresh thinking and methods of living out our faith. I hope many read this work in its entirety and take advantage of the Reader's Guide to promote group discussions about some of the suggestions in the text. I hope you find your time invested in the reading and understanding of this work as helpful and encouraging to your walk of faith.

ACKNOWLEDGEMENT

There is no doubt in my mind that the writing of this book would never have occurred without the love, support, and skill of my wife, Kirby. When I first expressed the idea of trying to put my journaling into a coherent message of a book, she encouraged me and expressed her confidence in my ability to do so even though I have never written anything for publication previously. She has been relentless in her support all through the process to include participating in my interviews of possible publishers of this text. Her editing skills have transformed my writing from an art form to a grammatically correct, coherent message. She has tirelessly acted as a sounding board to my ideas and shaped them with reason and a suitability for an audience that is perhaps not as schooled in all the church lingo as I am after being immersed in the community of faith for so many years. I have had no doubt that she is God's gift to me, but I never knew the detail and the preciseness of the match she is for me until the exercise of writing this book. I love her with all my heart and am as hopelessly devoted to her as she is to me. Thank you, God. Thank you, Kirby, my dear sweet wife.

INTRODUCTION

I am not a theologian, bible scholar or clergyman. I am one, like many, who has spent a large part of my adulthood deeply immersed in my faith. My time has been spent trying to achieve that delicate balance between vocation and avocation. My avocation has been for many years serving, teaching, counseling, and ministering in the evangelical community of faith. Let me define for the purposes of this writing as the evangelical community of faith as those Christian church denominations that ascribe to a generally common set of core doctrines with a strong emphasis on bringing new converts into their respective communities of faith. These would include but are not limited to such mainstream denominations as Catholic, Baptist, Methodist, Assembly of God, and Church of Christ just to name a few.

How does one become so consumed in matters of faith? Moreover, how does one spend so much of one's spare time doing unseen (prayer, meditation, reading, studying) at the sacrifice of things that are seen (sports leagues, social activities, general entertainment). Is the reason a result of some special calling in life or just being kind of crazy? I liken the experience to those storm chasers that go around the country trying to encounter, measure and document tornadoes and their effects. In their case we see the exhilaration of the chase and the anticipation of the intersection of natural and unnatural events. The results of those intersections can be visibly seen by buildings being flattened in a few seconds and cars being launched hundreds of yards in the air like projectiles. After which the location of such an intersection has been literally transformed into a completely changed environment. In my case, the chase has been in pursuing those events that I call the intersections of natural and supernatural events. Not supernatural like superman scaling a tall building or spiderman stopping a speeding train. No, I am talking about those events that change hearts and/or directions of one's life in an instant that can only be attributed to a force, a faith or an entity larger than ourselves. These intersections of the natural with the supernatural cannot be seen with the naked eye – but there is evidence left behind that they have happened. Relationships are repaired, behaviors changed, joy returned to a drained and empty soul are all evidence of an event that happens unseen to the naked eye. The author of the book of Hebrews calls that faith. "Now faith is the substance of things hoped for, the evidence of things not seen" (Hebrews 11:1). I call it God working behind the scenes if you will, covertly, silently declaring His willing involvement in each of our lives. This writing is to give testimony of those intersections of the natural with the supernatural as I have experienced them in my own life and understood them. I feel compelled to do so because I believe that recognizing these intersections is first, to understand that God is deeply involved in our lives whether we acknowledge it or not and second, that knowledge is the gateway to living a life of experiential faith that is vibrant, alive and fully aware of God's active presence in our lives! It is my experience that this kind of faith is rare in the evangelical church of today and desperately needed.

In order to begin the story of my faith journey I tried to think of the earliest evidence of God's personal involvement in my life.

It was at the end of what I believe to be my first day in the first grade. My class was being led down the cascading concrete stairs that connected the academic buildings to the bus parking lot. There we were released to board our assigned bus for the hour plus ride home. The joy of heading home after having survived my first day quickly vanished when I realized every yellow and black bus looked the same to me and I had no idea which one was mine. I can still remember the fear of being alone and the feeling of helplessness. I did what any first grader would do, I began to cry as loud and hard as I knew how in the middle of the parking lot. The next thing I remember is standing at the bottom of those concrete stairs looking up at the stream of kids running down to the parking lot in their green and white uniforms with bookbags and lunch boxes bouncing in the air alongside of them. Next to me was the nun in charge telling me to look for my brother. Evidently, I had composed myself enough to tell her I had an older sibling in the school, and she had assured me he would eventually show up. I can still visualize him bounding down those steps in full stride, careful not to misstep which would have been a huge embarrassment to take a tumble in front of his classmates. My heart was filled with joy at my sighting of him and I immediately knew everything was going to be all right now. Nothing was said to me by my brother that I can remember. He just grabbed me and loaded me on the bus with him and we headed home. I felt safe, connected and protected by my big brother. That connection that I felt to my brother that day was not fully understood at the time, but I knew I would be lost without it. It was the love of a brother. I still feel that same way more than 60 years later, even though we have been estranged for more than 20 years. I am not sure exactly what caused the divide. I have tried many times over the years to reconcile to no avail. I still hope the divide between us can be closed someday. I miss my brother. I feel the loss of that broken connection every day. Part of me is missing without it. I offer this experience with my brother to you as an example of an intersection of the natural with supernatural. There is nothing more natural than a relationship between brothers. What is supernatural is that that bond still exists between brothers regardless of the quality of the relationship. The feeling residing in each of our souls is the evidence of things unseen. What is unseen is what I believe is the bond that reflects the connection between us and our common Creator. I believe that even in the hurt of broken relationships we need to recognize the connection to our faith – not that God causes the hurt or even desires it – but it is that connection to each other that reflects our connection to God. Those connections of heart and soul endure over a lifetime, regardless of the circumstances and are not dependent on whether we physically see them or not. This past year our nation has come through a season that has recorded the worst pandemic in our recent history. Many of us have lost loved ones, friends and relatives. But we still feel connected to them. Far beyond our natural understanding our souls long for their presence. It is one of those intersections of the natural with the supernatural, connections that go beyond the grave and life as we currently understand it. Recently our president was speaking at the service of a fallen Capitol police officer killed while protecting the U.S. Capitol building. Speaking to the widow of the officer and his family he said, "they are gone but we still feel them." I suggest that is an intersection of the natural with the supernatural. The evidence of that unseen event is that hole in our heart. That evidence speaks of the presence of a power or a person bigger than our circumstances. That evidence I believe indicates the presence of God in the event. Once our faith is activated in that regard, we find our heart and soul lifted above our circumstances. We find ourselves in the realm of "the peace of God, which surpasses all understanding" (Philippians 4:7). The evidence of things unseen is our gateway to a faith that gets us through these moments whether we recognize it or not.

What follows is a compilation of similar life experiences I have had over the years. I choose to document these because throughout my faith journey I have strived to offer a simple explanation of faith to those willing to listen. My motivation has been and still is to communicate that faith is simply the evidence of things not seen, regardless of the form and function of that faith. We all exercise faith every day. Every time we step on a bus, train, or airplane we are placing our faith in the individual who controls that vehicle to bring us safely to our destination. Every time we sit in a chair, we put our faith in that chair to keep us off the floor. Every time we submit to surgery, we put our faith in the skills of that surgeon. Every time we elect a president of our country, we put our faith in that president to preserve and protect the constitution of our nation. My hope is that this discussion will help the reader to recognize faith as something we exercise every day. If so, then when those intersections of the natural with the supernatural occur in our lives, we will then recognize the faith that involves God. That is the faith that I have come to know and recognize working in my life. That is a life of experiential faith with God.

We live in a time when statements are made as facts that are critical to our well-being as a people and a nation, without the necessity of evidence. Evidence that can be seen, documented, and presented publicly are no longer a requirement to affect large segments of our society. This is a perfect time to present an argument for faith which is the evidence of things unseen. Hopefully, there will be a new willingness to accept a faith that does not require visible evidence. I hope you enjoy reading about my faith journey and it is helpful to you in some way.

PART 1
FAITH REVEALED IN A FAMILY

The search for the evidence of things unseen is a search to discover the elements of faith that exist all around us. Because this faith search involves those events that I describe as the intersection of the natural and the supernatural we must conduct our search over a continuum of both time and relationship. Because relationship begins with family, that is where we must begin. I will examine faith being revealed in a family first from the perspective of impact from generation to generation. Then I will discuss several areas of impact that are included in most families which are sacrifice, heartaches and what I call those wilderness experiences.

CHAPTER 1

Faith Revealed Generation to Generation

MUCH OF WHO WE ARE TODAY IS SHAPED BY THE INFLUENCES OF the generations of family before us. Much of what happens in the generations that follow depends on how well we prepare our children and their children for their future. That is not some philosophical view developed over years of research. That simply is the opinion of one who has lived long enough to see the impact on my life by past generations and the positioning of my children and their children for their future based on my generation. "Train up a child in the way he should go, and when he is old, he will not depart from it" (Proverbs 22:6). My experience seems to hold true to this proverb regarding both past and future generations of my family.

There were many aspects of my father's life that I would characterize as a paradox. He would often boast of the fact that he would smoke a pack of cigarettes a day and he had never been sick a day in his life. This seemed to be true as best as I can remember because he usually worked seven days a week, occasionally taking a family day off. I cannot remember him ever being sick until he abruptly died of lung cancer at the age of fifty-four. He did not complete the eighth grade but was determined both his sons would be college-educated and we both completed engineering degrees.

He was not a religious man but sent his kids to private parochial school. He took great pride in the fact that he was contracted to paint several Catholic churches in our area both inside and out. I remember one day when we were on a family outing, he took the time to show us a large church with an extremely high steeple that he had completely painted by hand using six-inch brushes. We were impressed! He would go to church on occasion with the family, usually on holidays. I always sensed his respect for the Catholic Church, which is where the roots of his faith were formed. He never talked about faith, God, or religion in general that I can remember. I was told that when he was in the hospital dying, he spent quality time with a young priest talking, confessing, and receiving communion. He was returning to his roots of faith when it mattered most. I learned much from my father, not necessarily from speaking because he was not much of a talker. He was not one to gather me near and share quality time together. But he never hesitated to take me out when I asked him and pitch batting practice to me until I had enough, regardless of how tired he was. He was a "do what I say, not what I do" guy. He said that many times to his teenage sons. He was stern and authoritative but there was no question about his love and devotion to his family.

My mom was more devout in her faith. Like my dad, she was raised Catholic. She too would attend church occasionally, usually with my dad. She faithfully taught weekly catechism classes to second grade girls at the local monastery for years. She was devoted to those little ones and enjoyed it immensely. Otherwise, she was devoted to her sons and her husband. Her world centered on them and their well-being. She was a licensed beautician when she met this GI home from the war on a train. At some point after that meeting, she and my father eloped. I remember my mom use to make some spending money by cutting the hair of the ladies in our neighborhood in our kitchen. I remember my mom endlessly working and filling the house with her Della Reese albums blasting away on the family hi-fi. Her devotion to my father was demonstrated by the fact that she never married or even dated another man after my father's death. She remained unmarried almost forty years, which was a longer time than she had been married to my father.

The impact our parents and past generations have on us is not realized quickly. Now I see that the foundation of my faith was constructed in those formative years with my parents. A reverence for the church and a sense of aligning one's life with God in some fashion was sprinkled throughout my life from an early age. Starting with baptism as an infant and the assigning of godparents who take responsibility for the care of the child's faith in case the parents cannot, a sense of faith is cultivated from a time before one is even aware of it. This experience is then soon followed by the ceremony of first communion, rich in pageantry and celebration which in my case formally initiated a connection of faith. Then, through the parochial school curriculum, that connection of faith was nurtured and cultivated through daily study in catechism and Bible history. Principals of faith such as "the Catholic church is the one true church" (as stated in our Catholic catechism at the time) are reinforced starting at this early age. It makes sense now, looking back, that if a child is of a compliant nature, this message resonates profoundly as it did with me. It was in the sixth or seventh grade that the boys were given a sales pitch to sign up for the priesthood. I believe the appeal was to sign up early so that we could then be directed to the appropriate high school a couple of years later to prepare us better for our devoted lives as priests. Whether my heart was tender at that early age with a willingness to serve God, or I was simply pressured to do so, I raised my hand to participate. I do remember I was a little skeptical in approaching my parents with my decision. When I presented the papers for them to sign to approve my request to enter the priesthood, they collectively hit their emotional ceilings at the same time, instantly! I do remember being surprised at the level of their emotion as they rejected the idea, while feeling relieved at the same time. I am grateful for all the support my parents gave me in forming a foundation of faith, but I am equally glad that they had the insight to know that their son really had no clue whether he wanted to be a Catholic priest for the rest of his life.

Looking back on that day I now recognize that event in my life as an intersection of the natural with the supernatural – evidence of things unseen – part of my faith journey being revealed. I attribute my parents' rejection of my priesthood request as nothing less than divine intervention. I believe that only the mind of God can discriminate the heart of a child in such resolution to know that this child would live a life dedicated to the pursuit of faith but would never have made it as a Catholic priest. I am not saying that the Catholic priesthood is not a noble pursuit, I am saying that is not the pursuit designed for my life. I know that now, I did not know it then. How could I know as a child the type of faith walk required for me that would take a lifetime to develop? Impossible, for I am only now understanding some of these events in my life decades later.

It was many years after the above events that I learned the reasons that my father dropped out of the eighth grade. My 90-year-old aunt, my dad's baby sister, filled in the details of the story during one of my last visits with her. The event that precipitated my dad quitting school had to do with a pair of shoes. My dad had tried out and made his eighth-grade basketball team with the requirement that each team member had to have a pair of basketball sneakers to play on the gym floor where most of the games were held. I am sure it was a luxury at that time to own a pair of shoes exclusively for the purpose of playing basketball. I find it hard to imagine as I look at my closet with its assortment of shoes for almost every activity, including walking, exercising, golf, beach, pool, and other activities. After his request for basketball shoes was denied, my dad must have been too embarrassed to face his peers on the team or else he saw no other long-term benefit to staying in school. The latter is entirely feasible given the fact that both his father and grandfather had immigrated from southern Italy in the early 1900's and would probably have given deference to work over education. I presume this based on my limited knowledge of my dad's relatives regarding education and skills. I do know that immigration documents list my great-grandfather's occupation as gilder, a craftsman who applied a thin layer of gold to furniture and household pieces. The 1910 United States census stated that neither my great-grandfather nor my grandfather could read or write. Given those facts it is likely they both saw more immediate value in working than pursuing any formal education and likely passed those priorities on to my father – one generation to the next. But that preference stopped with my father. He passed on to me the value and the necessity of an education. Why my father chose to change that generational tradition I do not know. That is one of the dozens of questions I have thought to ask him over the years since his death that never occurred to me to ask while he was still alive. Perhaps it was the result of a teenager working in New York City in the early 1930's with a partial eighth grade education or maybe it was because he survived campaigns in Africa and Italy as a medic during World War II. He tried chicken farming, working in factories, and other manual labor jobs before he took over his father's house painting business. Or maybe it was part of a plan orchestrated by something or someone larger than all the collective generations of my family. I defer to the latter because, when you continue the story of my education experience, you will read that my father and my grandfather attended my college graduation.

Three generations celebrating only the second college degree in our family, my brother being the first four years earlier. I believe that sometime during that graduation weekend, amidst all the celebration, the story of my father's basketball shoes must have come to mind either in my father or my grandfather, perhaps both. But it was never mentioned to me. Three generations celebrated one college degree with all that silently attached history of resisting or avoiding any formal education for two out of three of those generations. It is only when life events like this come into clear focus, sometimes long after the actual occurrence of the event, that one can recognize the backdrop of the divine architecture of life. This is the evidence of things unseen. The intersection of natural events takes on such significance that they can only be orchestrated with supernatural participation, in my opinion. The compilation of actions over generations that go before us implicate our lives in such dramatic fashion that it alters the effect and direction of our lives entirely. Some may say this is just the way things go, randomly occurring to the benefit or detriment of the individual. I believe such a plan can only be conceived in the heart and mind of God. The decision to embrace that perspective gives life to a dimension of faith in us that, if nurtured and cultivated, can grow to affect the generations that follow us. It then becomes a faith revealed from generation to generation.

Our decision to recognize that actions taken by the generations before us involve a divine oversight of God and introduces a supernatural component to a very natural occurrence of one generation passing to the next. Recognizing God's involvement in the shaping of our lives from previous generational actions gives rise to an experiential faith. A faith that can then be passed on by us to future generations. But how is faith revealed from us to future generations? Or in other words, how is faith passed on from us to our children and our children's children? Scripture is full of suggestions on how to share aspects of our faith like "A good man leaves an inheritance to his children's children" (Proverbs 13:22). But any of us who have lived for a while have witnessed how quickly any amount of inherited material wealth can be quickly dissipated through any number of economic, financial, medical, or personal events or simply just squandered. Also, there are any number of sacred traditions that can be attempted to be passed on as a measure of faith but as the old preacher once said, "you can't inherit your daddy's religion!", or in other words spiritualty cannot be handed down to the next generation. Each generation must adopt their own measure of faith as so desired. Below I refer to an example in scripture that we can employ that may help us transcend our faith experience during the passing of one generation to the next.

The event was the passing of my aunt, Celia Jinks, known to me as Aunt Sissy because she was the little sister of my father and her two other older brothers. She was our family's first and hopefully last loss to the coronavirus. She was spunky and a fun-loving lady. She is missed dearly. The following is a eulogy I wrote at her passing. She died in the hospital where she had been in intensive care for a short time. Because of the COVID19 restrictions her six children were not allowed to be with her when she passed, so they connected by phone as one of them shared this eulogy. I am so glad it was a part of her impromptu send off.

Eulogy to Aunt Sissy

I am so grateful to my cousins for interrupting their birthday celebration with my aunt approximately 6 years ago to unite me with her by a phone call. Aunt Sissy evidently had a desire to reconnect with me long after I had become consumed with living my own life. My last remembrance of seeing her was at my father's funeral in the fall of 1976 almost 40 years ago. When I finally came to visit her a few years ago, she invited the whole family over to share a macaroni and meatball dinner with me and my wife, Kirby. Unfortunately, she did not explain the house rule of a limit of two meatballs per person. Of course, I was starved for homemade Italian meatballs especially those that reminded me of my mother's and grandmother's. All was fine after I consumed somewhere between 4-6 meatballs until my cousin Rob showed up and asked "Hey, who ate all the meatballs?" My aunt was sitting next to me at her kitchen table and promptly cocked her thumb in my direction and said, "That guy!" That was my Aunt Sissy. The last time we spoke about four days ago she called me an "old goat". Same spunky Aunt Sissy that I remember from my youth. I will miss her dearly as I am sure all my cousins and family will even more so. But most of all I am filled with regret. Regret for years lost. Regret for times not spent together and things not done. But it occurred to me that those feelings fill each of our souls regardless of how good or bad our relationships are when faced with the finality of death and the grave. These feelings can be overwhelming at times and will not stop hurting no matter what therapy is applied. So how do we cope? I am no theologian or bible scholar. But a very familiar verse recently popped into my mind ...." Jesus wept." (John 11:35) Often described as the shortest verse in the bible I never gave it much thought until recently when the context of this verse occurred to me. It is quoted as Jesus is standing at the tomb of a dear friend who had died a few days before. The question that occurred to me was why was Jesus weeping knowing full well he was about to raise his friend from the dead? Why wasn't he trying to convince the family and friends who were blaming him for his friend's death that it was going to be all right, and that it wasn't his fault? Why was Jesus so emotionally moved that he was brought to tears? I believe it was because Jesus identified with the pain that all those folks felt when faced with the death of one that they dearly loved. I believe they were grieving over the loss of time spent with the deceased and all those other missed opportunities. They were dealing with the pain that you and I feel with the loss of my aunt who was your *mother, grandmother and all the many things she was to us. We feel it, I believe those folks felt it and I believe more importantly that our faith suggests to us that Jesus felt it then and still feels it for us today. What was Christ's reaction then, He overcame death with life. I believe He still does. I do not fully understand where Aunt Sissy is or what she is doing now but I believe she has overcome death and is in a good place doing well. I believe she is surrounded by love, your love, the love of Jesus and the love of others that have gone before her. I would not be surprised if she has connected with my Dad by now and has had enough time even to irritate Uncle Ronnie (just kidding). I think if we believe this to be a truth of our faith it will help make our present sadness a little easier and raise a wonderful hope for our future when we will see Aunt Sissy again!*

Death and the grave are natural experiences, aspects of which we will experience many times in many ways during our lifetimes and that we all will personally face one day. This past year alone besides my aunt I have had two college classmates and my cousin's husband all pass. There is not a clearer example that I can think of that illustrates the interaction of the natural with the supernatural. Death and the grave are a natural part of life whether we like it or not, whether we recognize it or not. What happens after I would argue is supernatural. The evidence of that is illustrated in the scripture referenced in the eulogy but I know by experience that if we apply our faith when facing the death of a loved one, it is possible to be lifted to a place of peace in our heart and our soul. That is not natural; I contend it is supernatural...the evidence of things unseen. God working in our hearts and soul whether we recognize it or not. So, what does all this have to do with the topic of this chapter? That is, specifically, what does this have to do with faith being revealed in us to future generations? Let us go back to the scriptural illustration in the eulogy to explain the connection.

Let us avoid any discussion of doctrine and assume that if one calls himself a Christian then he generally subscribes to some level of belief in Christ and His works. So, for the sake of argument, we are going assume all the details described in this scripture referenced in my aunt's eulogy to be true. Therefore, we can assume Christ shows up to demonstrate his sovereignty over death and the grave to prove his Deity to all of Lazarus's friends and relatives, but most of all to his friend who has been dead for several days. Or can we? Why would Jesus go through all this if He were quite aware of the fact that in a few days he was planning a similar but much more dramatic feat by rising from the dead Himself? Do you think He was searching for some extra media coverage? Or perhaps He wanted a practice run concerning control over life and death? Sounds a little silly, doesn't it? The only thing that sounds reasonable to me is that He was astutely aware of the pain that death and the grave causes to friends and family. His empathy is revealed by His tears. His faith is revealed in His words "Lazarus, come forth!" and "Loose him, and let him go." (John 11: 43,44) The first is a command to the object of his attention, the second is an instruction to those nearby that are watching. The first is directed to the dead man to rise, the second to the living to help the one that has escaped the grave. The evidence of the unseen is the joy in the hearts and minds of all those who witnessed the event then and all those who read about it now and feel through faith the victory over death and the grave. "O death, where is your sting? O grave, where your victory? (1 Corinthians 15:55)

Given the above discussion I believe the greatest gift we can give our children and our children's children is a belief in life beyond the grave, and to instill in them the belief that they are not alone in this journey and that we are in it with them for the long haul. It is relatively easy to stick a few dollars in the bank for future generations to spend after we move on. Too often, regardless of the amount we save to pass on to the next generation, it will be spent quicker than it took to save. It is also relatively easy to lecture our children about God and going to church, but it is just not highly effective. To plant the seeds of a life of faith is not a simple task covered in one simple conversation. To spread those seeds of faith to your children and their children will require taking advantage of those opportunities that come our way to share what we believe and know to be true through our own faith experience. I believe one of the most effective ways to do that is illustrated in our previous discussion of the biblical reference in John 11, Jesus at the grave site of his friend. If we live long enough, we all will inevitably have discussions with our children and perhaps our grandchildren about death, the grave and what happens next. I can think of no more effective message during those discussions than to assure them that it is going to be ok, and we will be together again. We do not have to understand all the theological arguments behind a statement like that such as the blood atonement of Christ and the propitiation of His death for the sin of man. All that can be left as an exercise for the reader. All one must do is to share his or her faith message from the heart. A faith message offers hope and encouragement. A faith message does not evoke fear or uncertainty. A faith message offers peace and understanding. A faith message is intended to build up someone else in their faith, not tear down. A faith message is not critical; it edifies. A faith message is constructed over time through an individual's faith experience. It will grow in depth and certainty as one's faith experience grows. The key to saying it effectively is that you must really believe it. One really cannot communicate faith in God and the things to come until one has experienced faith in God and has settled in one's heart how to approach the things to come. When a communication of our faith is effectively done, it invites an opportunity of those intersections of the natural with the supernatural. By that I mean those times and opportunities cannot be constructed in our timeframe by our making. We must wait for those opportunities to present themselves in a natural way. They will probably occur when you least expect it. They will only happen when it is supernaturally ordained when and where to happen. In those moments, if we respond in faith, we invite the supernatural to occur. That is, a communication of faith from one heart to another does not occur naturally. God must be involved.

I have been in the presence of someone facing imminent death three times. Once with each of my parents and once while I was a pastor. I will defer the pastor experience to the next chapter but simply say here that it was one of those moments of intersection between the natural and the supernatural. In the other two cases, I would not characterize anything about them but the natural passing of one generation to the next. My father was not in a coherent state when I last saw him. My mother was aware, but I was not sure if she heard me speaking to her. She would drift in and out of consciousness, mostly afraid when she was aware. I tried to communicate comfort and peace to her, to diffuse her alarm, but had no apparent effect. There were blocks of time when I talked to her while she was seemingly unaware. I remember at one point I told her that she was a good mother and that I loved her. Out of nowhere, without any change in her disposition or physical state she responded in a raspy voice, "I love you too." I believe it was the last time she communicated with me. These moments when we experience the transition of a generation are profound. One cannot intentionally prepare for them. We face them when we encounter them as best we can.

I like movies. I believe some capture unique experiences of life that we may or may not ever experience. I have never been to war but movies like "Saving Private Ryan" or "1917" give us a hint of what it was like. I worked with a Vietnam veteran who describes being there as an 18-year-old soldier so scared that he was sure he would never come home. I cannot imagine what that is like.

With that in mind let me offer a Hollywood example of having a discussion of life's generational transition experience captured in the 2002 movie "Signs" starring Mel Gibson and Joaquin Phoenix. The scene I am referring to is the one in which Mel and Joaquin are holed up in their home waiting for the aliens to overwhelm them. In those scary moments Joaquin (playing the younger brother) asks Mel (playing a former pastor) what he thought about life and death. Mel's response was something to the effect that there were two camps.... one group of people believe we are alone in this world... ... the other believe that there is someone watching over them and they are not alone. Joaquin's response was "I am definitely in the second group!" I use this only as an illustration of an event that was entirely impromptu, and the response was based solely on the faith experience of the participant (Mel being a former pastor).

So let me conclude this first chapter with a summary of my intent. Our faith journey begins in the family in which we are born. That family construct, world view and perspectives on faith are largely influenced by the generations that proceed our current family. I have illustrated those aspects of my faith influenced by that generational connection mainly through Catholicism. However, our individual faith experience does not determine in what form our faith legacy is passed on to our children and our children's children. I have illustrated that the opportunities and the effectiveness to do so are limited and highly conditional on our individual faith experiences. Let us continue with our examination of some other family experiences that will offer opportunities to grow and gain in our faith experience. Let us next look at the example of faith revealed through sacrifice.

CHAPTER 2
Faith Revealed through Sacrifice

WHEN I PASTORED, I WAS STILL WORKING A FULL-TIME JOB. ONE day I was asked by a coworker to deliver the opening prayer at her husband's retirement service from the Air Force because the chaplain had been called away on an emergency. Having done a similar function in a previous job I knew enough to keep it short, to the point and get off the stage quickly. I never took these opportunities for granted and viewed them as an opportunity to share my faith with a largely secular audience. I was shocked when I arrived at the ceremony site the next day to find a large mostly-filled auditorium, with a two-star general presiding over the ceremony. In military circles this was a big deal, and I began to wonder if perhaps I should have put a little more effort into my preparation for the event. When introduced I quickly read a verse of scripture, said a short prayer, and sat down. My whole contribution could not have been much more than 45 seconds at the most! You can imagine my surprise when the general took a few moments to thank me for opening the ceremony with such an inspiring message! Now if you have been around the military much you know general officers are not given to flattery and will not compliment an effort unless they sincerely mean it. Officers are leaders and they know any public comments they make are perceived as expected standards of performance and will be taken as guidance to their subordinates. The auditorium that day was filled almost entirely with military and civilian employees that were all his subordinates. My reaction to his words was to of course thank him but, in my mind, I was saying "Huh? What inspiring message?" At that point of my faith journey, I had spent many hours preparing teachings, sermons, and other comments for weddings, baptisms, and many types of other services, always striving to incorporate some type of meaningful message for the moment. This was the only time someone ever publicly described my efforts as "inspiring". So, what did I say that was so inspirational? The verse I read was "Greater love has no one than this, than to lay down one's life for his friends" (John 15:13). My prayer was a short one of thankfulness for the retiree's laying down his life in service of his country through the Air Force. No big inspiration there, but spoken in the environment of a military setting, with a mostly military audience, presided over by a military authority, it did have a divine effect. A moment of such spiritual harmony was struck for that group that it had the effect of a Billy Graham sermon! A natural event with a supernatural reaction. The evidence of that intersection of the natural with the supernatural was the reaction of the general. Such an interaction can pass as quick as it occurs but the impact stays residing in the heart, soul, and minds of those that recognize and embrace the moment. I have not forgotten that day; maybe it was meaningful for someone else besides me and the general that day as well.

Given the events in our nation over the past year plus, I would suggest that the laying down of one's life for his or her friends has become a frequent occurrence. With 700,000 plus deaths in the U.S. and approximately 5,000,000 worldwide from the coronavirus, the number of people laying down their lives for their friends is countless. Nurses, doctors, caretakers, service providers, and even common folk like you and me are risking their own lives to help those stricken by this virus. While the statistics that flash up on the nightly news become routine to the viewer, the act of laying one's life down for another never becomes routine. I believe that when someone willingly puts his well-being at risk for the well-being of another, he is entering an arena of faith and his faith is revealed. The evidence of things unseen or faith becomes very real to both the person at risk and the one trying to intervene on his behalf. What is occurring is an interaction between the natural with the supernatural, where life and death meet. It is an environment where the common response is a release of faith in the participants of the moment. That is why soldiers pray on the battlefield (never having been on one personally, I know I would be doing just that). And why people ask for prayer when seriously ill, regardless of their formality or maturity of faith. One does not lay his life down for another with the intent to find or increase his faith. One enters such a situation equipped with some measure of faith that has been developed prior to this event. What is revealed at a time like this is the measure of faith with which each of us is equipped. It is my belief that no matter how strong a measure of faith we have for these moments we will always be open to receive words of faith from those going through that experience with us. I will illustrate my belief concerning these matters with two experiences I have had. One as a pastor ministering to a man in his final hours on earth. The other was trying to help my cousin remotely while she was dealing with her COVID19 infection. They are different circumstances but they both relate to faith being revealed through sacrifice, the subject of this chapter.

My aunt was terminally ill fighting the COVID19 infection when my cousin received permission to visit her in intensive care. This was early in the outbreak of the pandemic and there were strict protocols to patient access and the number of visitors allowed in intensive care areas was extremely limited. I was surprised to hear my cousin was given permission to do so because it was my understanding only health care workers were permitted in this extremely contagious environment. Coincidently it happened that my aunt was in the hospital where another family member of mine had worked in administration for years and special permission was given to gain such access. As my cousin prepared to enter the intensive care unit, she was warned that once she came out, neither she nor anyone else would be permitted back into the unit. In other words, because my aunt was terminally ill, my cousin would be the last one from the family to visit before her death. Let me pause here to say that anyone who enters the intensive care unit, given the high degree of risk, must have an extreme measure of faith. My cousin had to be acutely aware that her visit was putting her life at risk. She was willingly laying down her life to be with her mom's last moments on earth. I am not sure that I would have had the courage to do that. Not sure many would. As my cousin gowned up, she was told the procedures being used to help my aunt transition from this life to the next comfortably. What was believed to be an imminent transition for my aunt, turned out to be anything but that. Whether what followed was an administrative oversight, a lack of proper medical judgement, or simply a case of the medical staff being overwhelmed and exhausted, what followed was described to me much later as a two-day nightmare. My cousin ended up staying in the intensive care unit with my aunt for a period of approximately thirty hours. Dressed in a surgical gown, gloves, mask, and shield for those hours my cousin watched her mom battle for her life, while wiping her forehead and face with a damp towel. I can think of no greater example of "laying one's life down" for another than what my cousin did those thirty hours. This does not minimize the selfless acts of soldiers, fire fighters, rescue workers, or health care workers. This just illustrates that anyone may be called upon to perform extraordinary acts of love. All that is required is for that someone to summons the courage to act. I am not sure I would have done what my cousin did. But it was not an unusual decision for her, because she had spent most of her adult life lovingly serving her mom. Those duties fell to her because she was the oldest sibling that remained in close proximity to her but more importantly, she had a capacity of love for her mom that was unmatched for such a time. Such sacrifice is never easy. It is just more readily available to those who have cultivated it over a lifetime. That is my cousin. I admire her and love her for it and for the person she is, a woman of faith. A faith different from mine and cultivated over a time and manner much different from my experience – a faith that is effective and meaningful to her life. There is no right or wrong way to cultivate faith. It is either meaningful or not. To my cousin her faith is a meaningful part of her life. In this case it was evidenced by her actions towards her mom's final thirty hours on earth. More importantly, my cousin's love for her mom was very evident to her mom. As my cousin entered the critical care unit that night, her mother greeted her with a faint smile and asked, "How did you sneak in here dressed like that?" Perhaps her mom was not fully aware, but I choose to believe it was just her spunky humor still showing through even at the end of her life. She was so glad to see her daughter, for she was being escorted from this life to the next with someone she loved right by her side. All that was required was someone to have enough faith to lay down her life for her. And my cousin showed up.

My aunt died April 24, 2020, a victim of the COVID19 virus. What followed over the course of about six weeks was a continuation of that nightmare for my cousin and her husband directly, and for the rest of the family by extension. When my cousin left the hospital there was no doubt in her mind that she had contracted the virus, although she would not experience any symptoms until a few days later. Her husband chose not to isolate from my cousin but decided to stay close to comfort his wife over the loss of her mother. Shortly after this time, I lost contact with them because they both became gravely ill. Around the first week of May we got word from my cousin's daughter that the family was extremely worried they may lose my cousin. Her husband, a big strapping guy, was extremely ill but seemed stable. My cousin was experiencing violent episodes of illness, effecting her general health in a very threatening way.

I will not suggest to you that I am some source of wisdom or monumental faith to handle situations like this one. I was not directly involved but still I found my heart, mind and soul preoccupied with the condition of my cousin. Not having any direct input or access to those suffering, I began to judge the actions taken by all leading up to the circumstances. Why did my cousin go in there? Why didn't her husband stop her? What were those medical nurses and doctors thinking? All these thoughts are quite natural but not extremely helpful for anyone. I believe that events that involve life and death issues are at the intersection of the natural and the supernatural. The only response helpful during these times is to summon from within our heart, mind, and soul any faith resource that we may have in reserve for the moment. In such cases I fall back on scriptures that have been most meaningful for me during the most difficult times. It has been my experience that when someone is extremely ill it is helpful to come alongside that person with some encouragement of faith because in all likelihood, they probably have exhausted their own internal resource of faith battling the illness at hand. So, I started texting my cousin scriptures. "Wait on the Lord be of good courage, And He shall strengthen your heart; Wait, I say, on the Lord." (Psalm 27:14); "Yea, though I walk through the Valley of the Shadow of death. I will fear no evil; For you are with me; Your rod and Your staff, they comfort me." (Psalm 23:4); "But those who wait on the

Lord Shall renew their strength; they shall mount up with wings like eagles, they shall run and not be weary, they shall walk and not faint." (Isaiah 40:31); "Fear not, for I am with you; Be not dismayed, for I am your God. I will strengthen you, yes I will help you, I will uphold you with My righteous right hand." (Isaiah 41:10) I would also add words of encouragement: "Praying for you!" "Stay strong, Cuz!" "I'm standing in faith with you believing for your healing!" Weeks later, after my cousin and husband were on the mend, my cousin shared with me that when she was the weakest and the sickest all she could do was read those texts repeatedly. Her emergency reserve of faith had run out, but these texts served as an oasis in her spiritual dessert.

When one lays his life down for another he walks into the environment where life and death meet, an intersection of the natural with the supernatural. There is no map available to navigate us through these events. All we have available to prepare for it is our faith. One is perfectly able to enter such a circumstance with little or no faith on reserve. It is not a requirement and I believe many people do. I offer the following insight for those who do. These events are filled with the unknown which causes fear. Faith is a valuable resource to fight fear. Faith is an antidote to fear. They are opposites that cannot reside in the same place at the same time. Fear follows when we feel alone and/or things are out of control. Faith says we are not alone and someone bigger than us is in control and has things covered. Fear comes when we do not know what is next. Faith says what is next is going to be all right. Fear says something bad is after us. Faith delivers the love of God into the moment. I highly recommend faith as an alternative for these moments.

But there is another type of laying down one's life for another that has a slightly different methodology, but a similar result. That is, whenever we invest our life in the lives of others, we are laying down our lives for them in a similar sacrificial manner. We are investing our time, knowledge, abilities, and sometimes resources into another person. Investing our lives in someone else is more common than risking one's life. Parents, grandparents, educators, coaches, pastors, ministers, health care workers and many others routinely invest their lives in others. Some do it out of love, some do it as a volunteer, some do it professionally making little or no money while some make a handsome living doing so. I am not suggesting that investing in another's life is the same context as expressed in John 15:13, but I think it can have a similar result in the revealing of one's faith. Let me illustrate my point with the following account.

As pastor of a small church for seven years I had the opportunity to minister to a terminally ill man. As I sat by his bed one afternoon, I watched several persons come by and express their love and gratitude to him for his contribution to their lives. Many tears were shed by these visitors as they communicated to him how meaningful his investment was to them. The man at this time was verbally unresponsive but was aware and I observed him being engaged with his visitors through eye contact and a slight turn of his head toward them when they spoke. I did not know this man very well and had only met him as a result of his wife visiting my church and inviting me to their home. He offered no evidence of church attendance, religious background, or faith in God during my several visits with him before he became unresponsive. But as I sat there next to his bed on one of his last days on earth, I felt an overwhelming impression that this man had done well with his life in the eyes of God. This impression conflicted with several principles that I had been taught about God and His judgement of our lives my whole life. Starting as a kid in the Catholic church, through my master's degree in religion, right up to my licensing and ordination as a denominational pastor, I had never heard of many exceptions in terms of what was acceptable to God in the conduct of one's life. Raised Catholic I was taught that unless you were in the Catholic church you were not one of God's chosen and were therefore unacceptable to Him. This was very upsetting for a young boy whose best friend was Protestant and therefore not in God's club with me. As a Protestant in different denominations, I learned that there were different requirements for what I refer to as jumping through different spiritual hoops to gain God's acceptability. The right prayer had to be said, or one had to be baptized the right way, or the right sequence of things had to occur all to gain acceptance into the Kingdom of God. But no matter what the denomination, all these faith communities required certain actions by the individual in order to gain acceptability in the sight of God and therefore by the church. All those years of understanding how to experience God and earn relationship with Him suddenly changed in me as I sat next to that dying man. I did not go there that day in search of any deeper understanding of my faith. I went there with the only thought being of one last opportunity to share my understanding of my faith with this man. As I sat there with this new sense of understanding welling up in me, simultaneously these counter arguments began to be rehearsed in my mind screaming "This can't be right!" It cannot be so!" "This is your imagination!" Soon this overwhelming impression that seemed to rise from my heart was pouring out through my soul and felt so compelling that I had to speak in the faith of the moment. I looked into this man's eyes and spoke the words to him that I believed that God was pleased with his life and that he had done well. At that moment all those arguments in my head vanished and I was never surer of anything I had done as a pastor than I was in that moment. In that moment when my eyes were locked with this dying man's eyes, I felt we were looking into each other's souls. At that moment I was filled with what I have come to know as the peace of heart that confirms when my actions become aligned with my faith. It is like the feeling I had as a small boy when I would go to confession and tell the priest my list of sins which was comprised of things like making my parents mad or holler at me. The priest would give me a few Hail Mary's to say and tell me to make a sincere act of contrition and to go and sin no more. I felt good, forgiven and that I had been true to my faith of the time. Now I felt the same, I had been true to my faith experience of that specific moment. What I believe happened that day was the peace of God I was experiencing by exercising my faith in speaking to that man at that moment somehow transferred the peace of God to that man when he needed it the most. Why? Because I am sure he was afraid. I believe he found himself in that intersection of the natural with the supernatural. I believe he was fearful. Who wouldn't be in those circumstances? I believe whatever faith reserve he may have had was long gone at that moment. He needed some access to a faith reserve so that he could receive the peace of God at that moment...the assurance that he was not alone, and everything was going to be all right. I believe that while he was realizing what was happening in the moment, it took me years to realize what had happened. All I know is that something happened to my faith from that day forward, the evidence of things unseen. I have also come to realize that what I experienced that day with this dying man was not that different from that experience that my father had in his dying moments. He too had invested his life in others.... me, my brother, my mother, and many of the extended family like uncles and cousins of mine. He too relied on the faith reserve of a young priest who came to the hospital that day to deliver the peace of God to my father as he transitioned from this life to the next. At that intersection of the natural with the supernatural faith was revealed as a result of a life invested in others. That priest that day used the ordinances of his faith to help my father, that day with that dying man I used the ordinances of my faith to help another man. Different expressions of faith, same result. I believe that in the intersection of the natural with the supernatural faith becomes a common denominator revealed in terms that are acceptable to God. They may not be acceptable comparing one church denomination to another, but I must ask the question, does that really matter? I do not think so.

I described the above experience to illustrate the point that faith is revealed through sacrifice, which is the subject of this chapter. That point may have been obscured in the telling of the experience so let me conclude by making that point clear. Our investment in the lives of others is a sacrifice made on our part that I believe yields dividends of faith in our lives. Those investments we make in other lives, those sacrifices we make because we can, not because we must, are of great value in the economy of God. Additionally, the giving of ourselves to the lives of our children, grandchildren and our extended family are required by us and, I believe of great value in the heart and mind of God. All the investments in lives made by us whether done out of love, obligation, benevolence, or just because we feel like it, all have great dividends to our faith. Those investments without mention of God, church, or religion. These are actions of faith that I believe bind us to our Creator whether we acknowledge it or not. Covertly, without our conscious cooperation, God sees the good things we do and the good people we are without us even realizing it. Pretty sweet deal! But really it makes a lot of sense. Why do we tape up those initial drawings of our children or grandchildren on the refrigerator for everyone to see? Those drawings where you cannot really discern what they represent but we love them and are proud to show them. Why? Because they are given from a heart of love to someone they love, expecting nothing in return. Why would God be any different? Acts of sacrifice that accrue over a lifetime given from one heart out of love to another who is the object of that love. I believe those acts of sacrifice are held in high esteem in the heart of God and He is incredibly pleased for all to know it.

There is one glaring omission from the argument set forth in this chapter with regard to the value of sacrifice in the growth of our faith. If sacrifice is as important to faith as is suggested, the obvious question is why? Why would any sacrifice of time, effort, and money that we make be held in any high regard in God's economy of faith? The answer is simple. The whole construct of our redemptive relationship with God is based on sacrifice. One specific sacrifice, that is. Christ's sacrifice of His shed blood and broken body just for you, me and for all. Our faith relationship with God has as its very core of existence the sacrifice of Christ. It only makes sense that any act of sacrifice on our part would evoke great favor in the mind and heart of God, the result being to grant more faith to those who sacrifice. After all it was His original idea.

CHAPTER 3
Faith Revealed through Heartaches

I HAVE SOMETHING IN COMMON WITH TOM CRUISE, DONALD Trump and millions of Americans – we each have been married three times. Practice makes perfect or in my case it took me three times to find the love of my life – more about that later. Being first married at the age of twenty-three, I quickly became a parent shortly before my twenty-fifth birthday. Looking back, I am not sure I was emotionally mature or financially prepared enough to be a parent for at least ten more years, but few of us are when we take the plunge. In fact, ten years later, I was already five years into my second marriage. My first marriage was noticeably short. However, it was long enough to have my only child, my daughter, whom I am incredibly grateful to have had even at such a young age. The marriage did not stand much of a chance to survive. We were married at a young age without sufficient time to really know ourselves or each other. Additionally, we had no idea what sort of life we expected to have together. As a result, the marriage ended suddenly and very badly. There were some difficult years immediately after the divorce. I had just begun my federal career so remained in the Washington, D.C. area while my ex-wife and daughter moved from Virginia to West Virginia, then to Ohio, followed by a move to Maryland and then finally back to West Virginia. It was there my ex-wife finally settled into a stable home and steady employment. The period of transiency lasted a couple of years which made visiting my daughter sporadic. Finances were always stretched thin. Soon after this last move, my first wife was killed in a single car auto accident in the mountains of West Virginia on Christmas Eve when she was twenty-six years old. After her death, my daughter came to live with me when she was a little over three years old. Going from being single person to being married is an adjustment. The transition to parenthood is again another big adjustment. But the transition from a married parent to a single divorcee to a single parent all in the span of a few years is quite another matter. It was an emotional roller coaster for all involved. I gladly took on the responsibility of raising my daughter, but I was not adequately prepared for single parenthood of a little girl. We survived through the grace of God, my mother pitching in to babysit on occasion, and a diet of hamburger helper with occasional nights out to a fast-food restaurant.

My daughter is married now with two beautiful children and they with my son-in-law are a vitally important part of my life. I love them dearly and cannot imagine what life would be like without them. On a visit several years ago, I was watching my daughter tell a story and she made an expression with a mannerism that reminded me of her mother. It gave me great pause because I realized in that moment no one else in the room would even be aware of that subtlety, including my daughter. I also realized in that moment I had never given any kind of credit to my first wife for anything to do with my daughter. All those years went by, and I ignored the fact that she gave birth to my daughter and was her primary care giver for the first few years of my daughter's life. Without her mother's contribution I would not have the beautiful daughter and grandchildren I have today. At that moment I felt an overwhelming gratitude to my first wife for her contribution. I also realized in that moment I had not really talked to my daughter much at all about her mother. In fact, I had not even mentioned her mom to her after that fateful night when she was a little child and had to explain to her that her mom had died.

I remember that night from over forty-five years ago as though it was yesterday. The plan was for me to meet at my ex-wife's home on Christmas morning to pick up my daughter so I could share part of Christmas day with her. When I found no one at home, the next logical place for me to inquire about my ex-wife's whereabouts was her employer's, a local veterinarian just down the road. It was there that I learned of the fatal accident. They had no knowledge as to whether or not my daughter had been in the car during the crash. I then proceeded to drive about fifteen miles to my ex-sister-in law's house not knowing the fate of my daughter. This was before the days of cell phones, and I had been on the road since sometime Christmas Eve and unreachable. Now as I drove on these same country roads that contributed to the fatal accident, there were no public phones, so all I could do was drive as quickly as possible. I had no active faith to call on. I remember being numb in my mind. I believe that was the only defense mechanism in my heart, mind, and soul available to cope with the fear of losing my daughter. My emotions were finally released when I found my daughter safe and well. All I could do was to sweep her in my arms and hold her tight as I wept. I later learned she had spent Christmas Eve there playing with her cousins and slept over. She had no knowledge of her mom's death. They were waiting for me to explain the events of the previous day to her.

Where does one begin such a conversation? At that stage of my life, I certainly did not possess any deep maturity about many aspects of life no less any meaningful ability to explain the death of her mother to a child. All I can remember is hugging her as long and as hard as she would let me, never wanting to let her go. Sometime later that evening, while holding her in my arms she asked me if her mommy was coming home. I said no, she had been in an accident, hurt her head, and went to sleep. I must have given her some assurance of coming home with me, but I do not remember doing so. As far as I can remember, we never discussed it again.

I am deeply ashamed of the fact that I had given no recognition of her mother's contribution to my daughter. I deeply regret leaving the responsibility of perpetuating her mother's legacy to my daughter's aunts and her grandmother. I did have the sense to foster my daughter's relationship with her aunts and grandmother and they did keep the legacy of her mom alive. I am incredibly grateful for that. I did recently confess these acts of omission to my daughter. It was an intimate, healing moment between us, divinely appointed and much overdo.

As I look back at this time of my life and try to understand the calculus of how these events fit into my journey of faith, it can be perplexing but somewhat predictable. Somewhere during my college years, the importance of faith in my life began to fade. The college I attended had mandatory church attendance on Sundays. Every Sunday, I found myself hiding in the upper balcony of the local Catholic Church resenting every moment of the service. That season fueled a general disinterest in God and hastened my retreat from faith. That was the state of my soul when I met my first wife in my first professional job after completion of my Air Force service requirement. It was an intense dating relationship, and we began living together soon after our initial date. The topic of marriage came up relatively quickly because it seemed the practical next step when it was time to renew the initial leasing arrangement we had. The logical choice was to be married in the Catholic Church because I had visited my first wife's Baptist Church in West Virginia while dating, and I wanted no part of that form of church service. I thought it to be insincere and not as reverent as the Catholic services. I remember we took the required classes for a couple to get married in the Catholic Church and that was the total faith investment we made in our decision. It makes sense to me now and I believe quite predictable that not having any active faith entering the important life decision of marriage would only contribute to the instability of that marriage. The marriage quickly evidenced itself as not only unstable but unsustainable. But the faith-less state of my heart was evident at the time because even as the tragic life and death events unfolded, I did not recognize any presence of natural events colliding with the supernatural. I do not remember any bitterness towards God, just being overwhelmed with a general sadness of life and determined to carry out my duty and obligation as a father to my daughter. I did not sense any divine plan through this set of events. It never occurred to me to bring God into these circumstances. It would not be until many years later that I would better understand the consequences that this portion of my life had in forming my faith journey for the rest of my life. I just remember that the best part of every day was those thirty minutes every evening during which I was able to sit in front of the television with my little girl in my lap, bath done, dinner done, and enjoying my time with her and thankful for it. What my faith tells me now is that God meets us exactly where we are. He never forces Himself on us. I was content for the time to be exactly where I was in my lack of faith. God was evidently good with that as well because there were no epiphanies or bolts of lightning appearing from the heavens. But all that would soon change. What I did not realize at the time was that God was working in my life. Not in an overt way, but covertly. At the time my focus was for the well-being of my young daughter. The provision and care for her consumed most of my waking thoughts apart from my time at work, but even then, in the back of my mind was the priority to fit the events of the workday into her schedule of needs. Little did I realize God's sovereign plan to change the focus of my world from an inward view of my needs and my issues to an outward focus on the needs of my child. Something that most dads eventually learn but I found myself on an accelerated course. The process changed my world view dramatically, giving me a deep sensitivity to the needs of those around me which no doubt shaped many of my life decisions going forward. That view was influential in such decisions as taking in my widowed mother when she could no longer make it on her own. It led to many years of lay ministry and eventually pastoring my own church. I believe those experiences were a result of those years that I thought were dedicated to formulating the well-being of my daughter as a single parent when actually it was God's way of forming the man inside of me for my path forward.

I had been a single parent raising a small child when I met a woman whom I thought was a perfect partner. She had been previously married as well and had two daughters, one within a year of the same age as my daughter and one a few years older. It seemed like a perfect arrangement. One daughter could be a playmate for my daughter and the older could be a built-in babysitter. Additionally, the woman could cook! It would be logical to think that having been through one bad marriage, I would be a little more deliberative and thoughtful about entering marriage again. Unfortunately, I cannot say I was. My dad had died a few months before my separation from my first wife and there was not anyone in my life to really advise or give me counsel in these matters. My faith was dormant in my soul and there was no church involvement in my life at that time. Subsequently, shortly after my thirty-first birthday I was married for the second time. Suddenly being the parent of three children, one a teenager, I quickly realized I was over my head regarding my domestic challenges. Regardless of one's age or maturity, I do not think anyone can truly be prepared for parenting in a blended family. I believe even in the best of circumstances a stepparent cannot have the equivalent bond as a child with a natural parent. I believe a stepparent's relationship with a stepchild must be based on mutual respect which is not quickly established and sometimes never. In my opinion, even in the best stepparent relationships the boundaries of that relationship must be recognized. I guarantee no matter how good the relationship is, at some point the child will declare that the stepparent is not his or her real mom or dad, usually during some disagreement. It happens. The truth is always inevitable. I also believe stepparent relationships will always have difficulty achieving the intimacy with the child as will be with the natural parent. That being said, my blended family was no exception. Early into my new experience I began searching for some much-needed support. For the first time in years, I became interested in returning to my faith roots. We had already enrolled my daughter and my youngest stepdaughter in private parochial school. It was logical to me that if the entire family was exposed to the Catholic Church, it had to be of some benefit. Routine church attendance had little effect in the family dynamic and the interrelationships began spiraling out of control. Soon, one particularly difficult evening occurred. I do not recall the specifics of the evening other than there was drinking, arguing and I realized my marriage was in deep trouble already. I did not know much about how to have a good marriage, but I already had the experience of one divorce and quickly recognized the symptoms of another. I found myself on my knees looking up to the night sky through my bedroom window and asking God if He was real, please help me somehow. That was the extent of my prayer. No epiphany, no response. At least not at that moment. That prayer was quickly forgotten until a few months later when I found myself attending a non-denominational Christian service on a Sunday morning as part of a business weekend offsite at a lodge in Pennsylvania. A colleague of mine who was a respected friend was speaking about his personal faith. The service ended much like the few Baptist services I had previously attended, that being with an invitation to come forward if you wanted prayer. In my previous experiences with these types of services, this is the portion to which I was most resistant. I felt like coming forward was contrived and a blatant display of attention. My Catholic experience always was quiet, personal, and not public. This time however, my response was different. I literally felt lifted out of my seat and escorted up to the front of the room where I embraced my friend. Many tears flowed from me, not knowing why. When I stopped crying, I had experienced a total release of all the anxiety built up through my desperation of the prior months with my marriage and blended family. Nothing physically changed but, in that moment, I knew everything was going to be ok.

Looking back, I now realize that was the beginning of a new faith journey for me. Up until that moment my faith was mostly informational. I had had years of instruction, teaching, and guidance regarding the religious celebrations of my Catholic faith. That was good but for whatever reason from this day forward my faith became experientially based. I felt something change in me! It was my first conscious exposure to that intersection of the natural with the supernatural. The evidence of the unseen was the change I had experienced within myself in an instant! There is nothing wrong with a faith such as I had had up to that point. It served me well up to the point when God knew I needed more. My own faith experience speaks to the fact that God meets us exactly where we are. If we want more of an experience of faith, it will happen.

Following the above experience, we were invited to my friend's Baptist Church. This was the start of a new beginning for the entire family. The church structure served as a vehicle to help me mature as a parent, husband, and a man in general. Over the next twenty-five years I attained a couple of different local church bible institutes certifications as well as a graduate degree in religion and counseling from Liberty University. I had many opportunities to teach, counsel, minister and eventually pastor a small church for seven years. As I grew in God's grace, I learned to negotiate many of the trials that occur in a blended family. Parenting in any circumstance has its extreme challenges, a blended family just has its own additional peculiarities. In my situation, added to the mix was the additional responsibility of taking care of my mother in my home because she could no longer make her own way. Ultimately things worked out in that all three children were accepted to college and all three eventually married. My mother was eventually placed in a retirement home and passed when she was ninety years old. Unfortunately, after thirty-five years of marriage many personal and relational issues with my second wife had been so compromised that not much of a relationship was left between us. At that point I had some severe health challenges and for the first time in almost thirty years I walked away from my faith. I felt spiritually dead and as though I was physically dying.

Although the marriage ended badly there was relational fruit from this blended family. My oldest stepdaughter became exceptionally close to me and my daughter. She has remained an active part of both our lives, and they treat each other like blood-related sisters. Known as Aunt Lisa to my grandchildren she has stepped into the gap to support my daughter and her children many times when I could not. She has been a close intimate friend to my daughter, and they have many common interests. To this day she still calls me Dad.

The following was written to the love of my life. We had been high school sweethearts and had reconnected after approximately forty-five years. At the time of the below writing, we had been communicating almost daily through text messages, email, and occasional phone calls. We had met for lunch once and both of us were involved in divorce proceedings after long marriages. She had three adult children, the youngest having passed a few years before our reconnection. She was living in Philadelphia, and I was residing on the eastern shore of Maryland. As Christmas was approaching the following was sent as my first Christmas present to her.

A Matter of the Heart

She always seemed to be aristocratic to him. Even as a teenager when he did not fully understand the meaning of the word he thought so. It may have been the small hint of a British-Canadian accent when she spoke. It was years later that he learned that her faint accent was a result of growing up with a father in the Foreign Service and as a child she lived in exotic places in Europe, Canada and others that were unknown to his experience. Maybe her aristocratic way was simply the way her long straight blond hair fell across her shoulders and bounced with her every step. Maybe it was the way she easily smiled and was always looking on the bright side of things. Perhaps it was her name, unusual from his point of view and much more elegant than Sue, Karen or Mary which seemed so ordinary in comparison. Who knows but he was certain she was of royal descent, although he never asked her. It was obvious to him, and he was certain it was equally obvious to the rest of the world. But he really did not care because it was a matter of the heart.

This certainty was renewed decades later when the social technology advances of the times permitted him to Google her name …. There she was …. Staring at him in all her regal elegance. "How could this be? Is it really her? Would she remember him? Was she married?" What he should do was not certain, but he realized what he could not do. He could not avoid the fact that he rediscovered her. He suddenly thought …. "Email …. what a wonderful way to reconnect!" He summonsed all his creative juices to craft the perfect communication. It had to be upbeat with a serious enough undertone that she would want to respond. He was surprised how easily it came to be written … now did he have the courage to press send? "How wonderful to hear from you!" she quickly responded. There it was …. Her elegance coming through every word! Instantly he felt 18 years old again! It was a matter of the heart!

He was running extremely late. First, he encountered early morning fog which made the going slow. Then the GPS lady told him to exit off the turnpike prematurely and he was now in bumper-to-bumper mall traffic. They were supposed to meet for lunch around 1 pm …. It was now almost 3. "Don't worry …. When you get here you get here…" said her text message. What a way to start off … He had wanted this day to be perfect … they had not seen each other in what a lifetime in experiences was literally…. Marriage, divorce, re-marriage, kids, grandkids, career, and dozens of moves. "This is insane! What is she going to think? I'm so nervous!" he thought as he parked in the lot outside her office building. "I'm in your parking lot ….. Meet you out front?" said his text. In a moment she appeared …. "Oh, my …. She's still so beautiful!" he thought. Their eyes met as they approached one another … "What should I say?" he thought. He did what came naturally …. He stopped and dropped his arms down in an open position towards her …. And they embraced. It was a matter of the heart.

We truly live in a wonderful age. He could sit in his office hundreds of miles from hers and routinely communicate with her. Text messages between business meetings were for those fun exchanges. Emails were for more detailed heartfelt messages. Selfies were used to capture what words could not adequately describe. Google earth allowed them to tour each other's current neighborhoods and to reminisce about places they had gone together many years ago. Not a perfect world for a relationship but they were content with it because of the current constraints of their lives. Happy to be reconnected, boundaries were understood and usually observed. He found he must discipline himself or else he would spend the day texting her. He settled into a routine limiting himself to one or two text exchanges a day. Often, he would drive to work telling himself he would abstain from texting her for the day just to give her a break. Often, he would give in by mid-morning inventing some excuse to text her like "What's on your list for Santa this year?" Boy …. How lame can one be …. She always responded cheerfully … never telling him to stop bugging her. He longed for those exchanges when they would get caught up in some topic and before they realized it, the afternoon was gone! He looked forward to going to the office knowing that it was a good chance that he would hear from her sometime during the day. On the rare occasion he would take a risk and text her during a weekend or day off. He was always worried that those exchanges would put her in an awkward position. It was a risk to the existence of their relationship which had remained largely covert at his insistence. He wanted her all to himself … he was not willing to share her … for now she was ok with that, but he knew it bothered her. There was nothing else he could do …. It was a matter of the heart.

It was 3 am and he was awake. He had been awake for some time and he was thinking of her. She occupied more and more of his thoughts …. in the office, during his long commute, watching TV …. and yes, during those sleepless nights. He remembered something her mother had told her. "It's the middle class that struggle through their relationships. The rich buy their way out of tough situations. The poor simply ignore them. The middle class are stuck to fight their way through the tough times." (His paraphrase … …. he could not remember her exact words.) He thought "This is going to end up bad" as he laid there. "Someone is going to get hurt …... it's probably going to be you, Bubba!" "Wait a minute! You got this all wrong!" he argued with himself. "After all - this is a matter of the heart! That is right! Matters of the heart are not intrinsically good or bad … they are what they are. They are created in the image and fashion of the heart in which they reside. If they are governed by a desire not to hurt or do harm, they are free to lift, encourage and give hope to those that give rise to them." Suddenly he *felt encouraged and hopeful. He quickly fell into a deep sleep and slept soundly for the rest of the night…. After all it was a matter of the heart.*

Who can say what lies ahead is good or bad especially when it involves a matter of the heart? These issues do not play by the same rules. In one instance they may cause one ordinary person to attempt something extraordinary. In another they may render the most routine task impossible to do even though it has been done hundreds of times previously. These matters cannot be planned or predicted, only experienced. The deeper one goes in these matters the higher the experience gets. As these matters grow in one's heart the greater the joy but the risk of great sorrow increases. They are a paradox, hard to live with but even more difficult to live without. He counts himself fortunate to have encountered this heart matter during this season of his life. This season for him has been dominated with despair and disillusionment. But this heart matter has changed all that … it is now a season of new and hopeful experiences! What he has learned is that one heart matter can affect other matters both heart and not of the heart. He is deeply indebted to that island girl that has so miraculously reconnected with his life. Whatever the outcome will be, he is sure he is a better person because of it. His only desire now is that he hopes she feels the same way.

My wife and I will soon celebrate our fifth wedding anniversary. We have lived those words that I previously wrote to her "that one heart matter can affect other matters both of the heart and not of the heart." Our lives have changed dramatically. My wife and I have rediscovered a love that we had only glimpsed when we were teenagers. Then it was never more serious than "necking" in my father's car after a movie, but it was a tender love towards each other that neither of us had experienced since. It was rekindled in our hearts and minds soon after we met again many years later. This heart matter has broadly affected all areas of our lives as well. My wife is the grandmother to my grandkids that they have always wanted and needed, and she is the "Grammy" she always wanted to be. Some may speculate that I have lost my faith, but I would say that my faith has not been lost but profoundly changed. A faith that was formally constrained by denominational doctrines and teachings has been released, reformed and proven to me to be very personal. It is now an intimate faith, customized according to the experiences that have shaped it. Countless times while my wife and I were negotiating our way through the issues of life that entangle one after previous marriages of many years, I would pray for God's guidance. I gave my faith a chance, giving it permission to circumvent events, change my path or stop the direction my heart was leading me at any time and in any way. Each time that I surrendered to my faith by literally praying in my heart for God to show me the way, the path towards a future with my wife never changed but often was accelerated by events. One might say this is all circumstantial and things happened to work out with a little imagination and cutting the corners where faith conflicted with personal desire. My response would be, perhaps, except that my faith experience has always been a matter of the heart starting that day in that non-denominational service when my faith changed from head to heart. I do believe faith has always been designed to be a heart matter. Scripture talks about the heart often. "Hope deferred makes the heart sick." (Proverbs 13:12) We all have felt that in our lives at one time or another. In so doing we all can attest to a simple understanding that the heart as referred to in scripture is more than an organ that pumps blood. As important as that function is to our life, it is not just that. It is the seat of our desires, emotions and will to mention a few of the heart's attributes. I characterize it as being more the soul of our being, although some may disagree. We all know what it means for our hearts to be broken, weary, exhausted, and sometimes as though they are dead. It means we are no longer able to function relationally with

the Blue Ridge Mountains without shelter, shower or shave playing soldier. We slept in the elements with only a sleeping bag with temperatures hovering around freezing at night. I quickly learned to stuff everything in the sleeping bag with me after the first night. I remember violently shaking while eating breakfast after that first night because I had to wear my boots while still frozen. One year the group I was with got lost while on night maneuvers. We stumbled around in the dark until we happened to run across another group to set us in the right direction. None of these experiences prepared me for what I call a true "wilderness experience" that I would experience many years later.

Most of us have had or will have a time in our life when we feel overrun by wild circumstances that were neither planned nor ever expected to be encountered. These events are like that first weed that appears either in a garden or driveway that is ignored. It seems that overnight this weed has multiplied and despite one's best efforts to mitigate its growth it becomes completely out of control. Soon what exists is no longer anything like what was once there. Similarly, I characterize a "wilderness experience" as an experience when those things we have labored over, prayed for, and prioritized in doing, suddenly change. Whether it involves a circumstance, a relationship or both, suddenly what was, no longer exists in the same way. We are in a "wilderness experience" when suddenly what we know to be, no longer bears any resemblance to anything we knew before, not sure how things changed so dramatically and with no idea how to get out of the new circumstance. In those "wilderness experiences" of life we sense peril; physical, emotional, financial, spiritual, or maybe all of those at once. Because of that sense of peril, we feel some action is required to survive or else we may not, but we do not have a clue what to do. That is the "wilderness experience". We then realize that this is a different circumstance because all our usual antidotes no longer work - alcohol, working out, arguing, or even prayer. Reading the bible has no effect and any counsel sought seems missing the mark, not quite fitting our circumstance. Welcome to the "wilderness".

My wilderness experience came when I thought I had seen most of life's difficult challenges. All the kids were grown and settled. I had retired from my federal career. I had closed the church I started and pastored for seven years. Having moved to what I thought was my place of retirement, I took a position teaching math in a public high school to cover the transition into retirement. Having taught high school math previously for three years, I was congratulating myself because now I was near the beach with easy access to fishing and golf. How hard could it be to teach a few classes with all summer to enjoy the sun and fun of the new location? Then my world turned upside down. While teaching on the mainland away from the beach I discovered the area to be in a socially economic depressed area. Poverty was a way of life and new teacher instruction included ways teachers were to be sensitive to the student's needs. However, no training could prepare a novice teacher for the experience. Teachers were often required to visit students who were suspended to try to keep them from falling too far behind. When one of my students was visited, she was found to be living in a small trailer with no heat and with several combined families. It turned out to be the most difficult job that I had ever had and that I hated the most. Barely surviving two years at the school, I quit before I was fired, never having quit anything in my life before! That is not meant to be a boast but simply to say I am not one that easily gives up on something. Particularly this plan because it was not conceived without serious thought and preparation. In order to teach in a public school, one had to be licensed by the state. In my case it required taking several graduate courses in education, along with reading comprehension and writing skills tests. For me it meant passing the math comprehensive exam which covered every math

(Algebra, Geometry, Trigonometry, Calculus and Statistics) most of which I had not been exposed to since college. It took me four times before passing the exam by only two points. With that kind of emotional investment into this teaching experience it was exceedingly difficult to walk away from it and I left with a feeling of failure. After some extensive searching I was able to find an engineering job; unfortunately it came with a daily two-and-a-half-hour round trip commute. Within six months of starting my new job for the first time in my life I had a health crisis. The next four years would require two major surgeries and two minor surgical procedures requiring large blocks of time not working. It was in the middle of this health crisis that my marriage of thirty-five years crumbled. There were signs over many years, but I always attributed them to some complication that needed to be worked through over time with patience. Even in the best of marriages there are relationship issues. But I believe scripture supports the concept of a breaking point in marriage. In Mathew 19:9 Jesus emphatically states his case against divorce but with a caveat. I believe there are boundaries of intimacy in a marriage that if violated often enough will kill the relationship, regardless of the maturity and depth of one's faith. That is the "wilderness experience". Once in the "wilderness" there is no more accommodation for the relationship, it becomes survival mode only for the individual. The union that was, no longer is the same. Is it possible to restore a marriage that has reached this point? I know on rare occasion it is. But any recurrence of this kind of a breach in the relationship will, with little doubt, finally end that relationship. This I know to be true. Additionally, besides being physically and emotionally drained at this juncture, I felt spiritually bankrupt. My faith had been an integral part of my life for many years but now it was no longer present that I could tell. I no longer had any interaction with people of faith. Additionally, being consumed with physical, financial, and emotional worries, I no longer thought about spiritual things and felt as though I had lost all connection to God. I felt alone, like I had lost my way and did not know how to get out of the predicament in which I found myself. I was deep into my "wilderness experience".

Perhaps the most amazing thing I have learned through my journey of faith is that I believe God never stops working in our lives. Sometimes specifically in such certain terms there is no doubt that you are experiencing divine intervention. Sometimes His work is so dramatic it cannot help but evoke intense emotion. But most times I believe God works unaware by us and we only recognize God's involvement after the fact, sometimes years later. It is on those occasions and only after we have labored through the trial, that the intersection of the supernatural with the natural becomes revealed to us. "Ask, and it will be given to you, seek, and you will find; knock, and it will be opened to you. For everyone, who asks receives, and he who seeks finds, and to him who knocks it will be opened." (Mathew 7:7,8) Funny how that works. So it is with the "wilderness experience". Let me illustrate with scripture to make my case. We find in both the books of Isaiah and John the account of the prophet John the Baptist described as the "voice in the wilderness". The specific context was that he was the announcer of the coming Messiah, Jesus. Isaiah 40:3 tells that the arrival of Christ will be accompanied by a physical shaking up of the environment - actions like highways in the dessert, mountains flattened, valleys filled, crooked places made straight and rough places made smooth. Sounds like a Federal Highway project through the Rocky Mountains. But the account in John 1:23 makes direct reference to the account in Isaiah with only the reference to the "voice in the wilderness" and a straight way to the Lord being made. Obviously, the Isaiah account is a metaphor. And the obvious theological argument is that what was a difficult path to God is now being made easy with Christ's arrival.

I totally get that and stand in agreement with the theology. But here is where my faith has been expanded from information and doctrine about God to my experience with God. If we are talking about a metaphor of faith, then how about God being the voice crying out to us into our "wilderness experience"? The prophet Elijah was going through a "wilderness experience" of his own. In 1 Kings 19:11-13 it states that he could not hear God in the wind, in the earthquake, or in the fire but in "a still small voice". I believe we cannot hear God's voice in our "wilderness experience" because we are fighting for our lives and we are not listening. The relational winds are blowing with hurricane force. The emotional and sometimes financial foundations of our lives are shaking like an earthquake beneath our feet so violently that we are unable to take even a step forward. The angry fire of bitterness consumes our souls, leaving room for nothing else. But somehow, we survive and suddenly we begin hearing God's voice again, as did Elijah in the cave, "What are you doing here, Elijah?" In God's grace and his time, we begin the introspection, the self-evaluation necessary for the first step, then another. Suddenly the voice in our "wilderness" begins the transformation of the relational landscape of our lives. Those dry, desert like relationships start to have new paths made to them. Those areas of relationship that have been bent and crooked are made straight. Those relationships that have been separated through mountains of time and valleys of neglect are now accessible once again. As a result of my wilderness experience my relationship with my daughter, my grandchildren, my son-in-law has become watered, renewed, and saved from what was distant and dry. My relationships with extended family in other states that were hidden by time and circumstance have been renewed. My relationships that go back to high school and college, with friends that were my closest friends for many years that had been forgotten, have been restored like there was never a pause in relationship. But most of all

I am married to the woman that I have no doubt was in the mind of God all along. Yes, all this is a difficult construct. But new highways are not built without moving a lot of dirt out of the way. Roads are not straightened without changing the landscape. But only when the reconstruction of our life is complete, one realizes that it only could have been accomplished by the hand of God. As the prophet said, "Then the glory of the Lord shall be revealed, and all flesh shall see it together!" (Isaiah 40:5) - the evidence of things unseen in our relationships and our "wilderness experience."

The "wilderness experience" is not something to be sought before it happens or to be edified after it is over. My purpose in documenting my experience is to be a voice to say if it happens to you or someone dear to you, just hang on and watch God work. You might not see any evidence of that now and may not for a while. But when you finally get to that point of stillness in your soul just listen for that "still small voice". I believe with all my heart it is there. It is the evidence of things unseen, God working in your life.

PART 2
FAITH REVEALED IN A COMMUNITY

Our search for the evidence of things unseen continues to be a search to discover the elements of faith that exist all around us. In Part 1 we focused our search regarding the family. Our generational family and the experiences we have in our families all have an impact on the formulation and emergence of our faith. After family, perhaps the most significant influence on the development of one's faith is the local community. One cannot talk about faith without discussing the direct and implicit effect community has in the formulation of our faith. I recognize that one's community is much broader than the church we attend. I am certain that some aspects of our local community such as schools, civic organizations, social groups, and government will all have some effect on our formulation of faith, but I am not qualified to speak to any of these aspects. Timothy P. Carney's states "Religion, like every worthwhile thing in life, needs community." Carney goes on to say, "The three things here – family, faith and community – are so intertwined in human nature that all three must be understood as both causes and effects in mutual reinforcement."[1] Part 2 of

---

[1] Alienated America by Timothy P. Carney, p.141, HarperCollins Publishers, 2019.

this writing will address the effect the church community has on our faith. I think it is obvious, that the church community with which we associate ourselves has a direct effect on our faith in terms of the doctrine and denominational customs we embrace as part of that faith. Having been exposed to several denominational views in the evangelical community of churches, I realize that each has an implied effect on one's faith. My experience has included four different denominational churches and one independent church, each a part of the evangelical community of churches. Consequently, one may characterize my faith as eclectic. I like to think of it as evolved. That is, I still ascribe to and believe in most of the doctrines of the evangelical church at large, with some what I would consider minor exceptions. But my preferences of custom, style, and methods in acting out my faith have changed significantly. For example, just the writing of this document has been a tremendous exercise of my faith and unlike anything I have done previously in all the years of my faith journey. Consequently, I would characterize my faith now as a hybrid of the faith I once had. It is a result of a faith journey over time and many observations of those intersections of the natural with the supernatural. I believe this hybrid faith is an evidence of things unseen, specifically in my life. An example of God working in us, in this case fashioning a fresh faith for me. I have categorized my observed implied effects of faith by the evangelical church in the following four general areas, each to be discussed in a subsequent chapter: Consequences of Faith, Evolution of Faith, Certainties of Faith, and Integrity of Faith. I hope what follows is of value to you.

CHAPTER 5

Consequences of Faith

~

The fruit of the righteous is a tree of life, and he who wins souls is wise."

(*Proverbs 11:30*)

THERE ARE COMMONALITIES AMONG ALL EVANGELICAL churches, but perhaps the most significant has to do with the label of being "evangelical". While there are doctrinal differences as to the how and the why, we all embrace evangelism, hence the label. The purpose of evangelism is simply to bring new members into the church or converts into the fold. As noted previously, my faith journey began as a Catholic at an early age and Catholicism remained exclusively my faith experience until my early thirties. From that point until now, while occasionally attending a Catholic service with a friend or relative, my faith experience has been in Protestant churches. My faith journey in the Protestant church has been almost equally divided between Pentecostal and Non-Pentecostal, with my current preference being the Pentecostal church. Those last few statements alone would probably make a lot of evangelicals nervous but that has been the nature of my faith journey, not by plan but by experience. The reason I am making these distinctions in the evangelical churches is because in my experience the "consequences of our faith", which is the subject of this chapter, are or can be different in the various evangelical communities. The "consequences of our faith" are simply the outcomes of our faith fostered and shaped by our respective communities of faith. I think that is an important distinction to be illustrated to avoid any suggestion that all evangelical churches are the same.

As mentioned previously, I had the benefit of being sent to a private parochial school from first through eighth grade. The school was graced with a small contingent of live-in nuns and an ornate chapel. We were required to attend routine chapel services which included a choir of nuns singing a selection of hymns. The combination of limited student attendance, the chapel's high ceilings and the nun's wonderful voices made every service feel like we were in heaven, or at least close to it. Even a small kid was left with the impression that the environment somehow changed when those specific elements of our faith were introduced to it. Looking back on my years of faith as a Catholic, I believe the overwhelming consequence of that faith was a sense of reverence towards God, the things of God and our faith in God. These things are not to be approached in a cavalier or a matter-of-fact manner. That has been a consequence of my faith as a Catholic that has stayed with me the entirety of my faith journey. That was certainly evident when years later my wife and I visited the Vatican. Standing a few feet from the Pieta, walking the cavernous halls, and watching clergy carry out their priestly functions required a respect and reverence that came with that environment of faith. This was a consequence of my faith learned as a child in a Catholic chapel.

My introduction to the Protestant evangelical faith was through the Baptist denomination as described previously in this text. In the Catholic Church, evangelism was inherent. That is,

Catholics are usually born into the faith starting with a baptism usually during infancy arranged by the parents. Exceptions to the rule are conversions later in life, similar to my wife's experience which was to be baptized at Siasconset Union Chapel as a teenager, at the insistence of her father. The emphasis on evangelism was quite different in the Baptist community of faith that I entered in the early 80's. There the emphasis was on personal evangelism and church members were instructed and encouraged to share their faith in a personal way, inviting people into the fellowship of the church and the faith. Any successful results were shared in public services and both the member and the accomplishment were edified. With this in mind, a new member like myself was always looking for opportunities to exercise my faith and to be accepted into the church community as a person that was serious about his faith. One day, in the government office in which I worked, a young secretary had a stroke. Viewing this as an opportunity to share my faith, I reserved a government conference room, called a prayer meeting for the secretary on government time, and used government resources to create a flier to announce the meeting. The results were as expected during such a time. The secretary was popular, everyone was concerned about her, and the conference room was packed, standing room only. I prayed, shared my faith, and concluded by inviting everyone to my church. I phoned in the results to my pastor who was elated and shared the whole episode with the entire congregation on Sunday. I felt that I had just been used by God in a great way and all the attention made me feel like a rock star! The truth of the matter, as I see it now, is that I doubt God was in any part of that event. My pride and motivation to be accepted by a community that was important to me was driving the entire caper. The good news is the young lady fully recovered; I now believe that had nothing to do with my efforts. I view that day now as unethical at best and an incredible waste of government resources. It was probably an act of God's grace I was not fired for pulling such a stunt. But that effort changed something in me. It engaged me in a spiritual dynamic with which I was unfamiliar at the time. Now I view such events as that wonderful blending of the natural with the supernatural – some combination of the two intersecting in some miraculous way. That is what I see when faith enters our living experience. The truth of the matter is that all of our faith is inadequate at its best, in the context of trying to know and understand the mind and heart of God. All we can do is to try and step out in faith. That was the consequence of my faith experience from those initial years in the Baptist church. It gave me a hunger to step out in my faith and experience God. Over the next twenty-five years or so from that day in the government conference room, there were many similar events such as that one. No, they were not on government time or using someone else's resources. They were in my spare time including early mornings before work, late nights, most weekends and any idle moments I had. I was consumed with the chase of finding the intersection of the natural with the supernatural, just like those storm chasers mentioned earlier.

I also believe this is the consequence of faith that is described in Hebrews 12:29. "For God is a consuming fire." My faith experience over the years bears witness to the context of this verse. That is, God is a change agent. I believe God's target of reform is to change us from religious to spiritual. God is not the inventor of the doctrine that accommodates the peculiarities of our particular community of faith. Doctrines are man's interpretation of God's intent. God is in the business of changing hearts, minds, spirits, intents, and lives. His consuming fire is not physical but spiritual. His process results in changing our judging into accepting, our being critical into being gracious, our bitterness into forgiveness, our anger into joy, our war into peace, our hate into kindness and even love if we let Him. These are the consequences of faith from God's view, regardless of our community of faith. These are the evidence of things unseen.

The consequence of my faith journey in the Baptist church was to light the fire of my faith journey. The consequence of my faith journey in the Pentecostal church was to release me from the regimen of faith into having grace in my faith. Regime requires our faith to be lived in defined routines: reading the bible every day or the whole bible every year; attending church whenever the door is open; giving, doing and showing up routinely. Grace requires just being and recognizing that we all exist in various states of grace under God's eyes. Grace means to look at each other with an understanding that we are all imperfect and trying our best. Grace means an absence of judgement of people and the events of our lives. Grace is humility and thankfulness for our lives regardless of circumstances. Grace in faith says people are no longer objects targeted to change and to conform them to my way of belief. Grace puts us all on an equal playing field when it comes to God. We are all just trying to get along in life so let us do what we can to build each other up and help when we can. Grace in my faith constrains me to speak less and understand more...to look at a person as another living soul and be open for opportunities to communicate the things of God if given an opportunity.

A few years ago, my wife and I were having lunch with my two new stepdaughters. Each are young professional ladies, with advanced degrees and successful in their respective professions. It had been a difficult transition for them, and this was the first informal attempt at welcoming me into the reconstructed family after their mother's marriage to me. It was towards the end of a quite pleasant time of chatting and eating when I was suddenly asked by the eldest "Are you a religious man?" I was stunned by the question because we had not even come close to talking about anything of faith or God the entire time up to that point. Both girls had been educated in a private Quaker elementary school but now as young women they were not actively part of any faith community. Should I respond by summarizing my 25-year faith journey? Should I mention my master's degree in religion? Should I highlight the key doctrines of my faith? I would have possibly chosen anyone of those answers at some earlier time in my life – but not at this point of my faith journey. "No, I am not religious, but I like to think I am spiritual" was my response. "I like that" was her response with a smile. I believe our statement of faith should try not to be intimidating in any way. It should be constructed in such a way as to always leave the door open for future discussion. For a long while, I did not think that way. I believed a full-throated defense of one's faith should be offered regardless of how receptive the audience may be. That is not me, now, thanks to the consequence of my faith in the Pentecostal community of faith. Fast forward a few years to a recent Christmas celebration with my wife and these two same stepdaughters. It was the first of its kind and it was wonderful. Lots of open discussion, laughing, enjoying each other's company around the family room fireplace. We did not talk about God, faith, or religion. But it was a first step in feeling the oneness of a new family construct. It was peaceful, lovely, and noted by both young women as an experience they would welcome in having again. The evidence of things unseen – God's work in reconstructing a new family relationship.

Let me summarize by repeating the "consequences of our faith" are simply the outcomes of our faith fostered and shaped by our respective community of faith. My intent is not to pass judgement on these outcomes, they simply are what they are. My outcomes are a collection from different faith communities resulting in the construct of my faith today, which I earlier referred to as a hybrid faith. This is neither preferred nor not preferred, neither is it liked nor disliked. It is just the nature of my faith, as is each of ours, as it relates to the faith communities in which we have been a part. The value of this discussion is not to do a comparative analysis of the various denominations in the evangelical church community. The value is to shine a light on the distinctions that may not be so visible to the world outside evangelicals. Evangelicals have similar beliefs, but we do not all act out in those beliefs in a similar manner. I bristle when I hear a political analysis assigned to "evangelicals". It has about as much meaning to me as an analysis assigned to senior men who are balding and overweight! There is about as much similarity in the first group as there is in the second! I am quite convinced that there would be many evangelicals who would disagree with many things I have said in these pages about faith, God and my views on both. But I also believe there are many who would agree. Regardless of our differences, we are all grafted into the same vine as noted in John 15. We are different branches, bearing different fruit. That might be stretching the metaphor, but I think that is acceptable considering there are over 5,000 different types of grapes to make red wine alone. We are all part of a diverse vineyard. In God's eyes we all produce a wonderful blend of a fine wine.

CHAPTER 6
Evolution of Faith

REPENTANCE FOR THE REMISSION OF SIN IS A SCRIPTURAL principal practiced by the evangelical community. As a child in the Catholic church, I remember going to confession with a laundry list of sins comprised of such atrocities as "making my parents angry" or my favorite "making my parents holler". Coming from an Italian family hollering was a time-honored tradition and you can bet there was a lot of it! My grandparents hollered at each other, my dad hollered at his brothers and of course my parents hollered often at my brother and me! I do not remember specifically when I realized that my sins had matured and I graduated to a more serious confession, but I am sure that happened at some point. There is a natural maturing to our faith, or progression if you will, in all our faith experiences. Scripture validates this principle as well. "For in it (note: referring to the gospel of Christ) the righteousness of God is revealed from faith to faith." (Romans 1:17) This implies that faith is not only continuous, but also it is a sequence of events on that continuum of time. In other words, our faith journey is marked at separate and distinct times with additional events. I like to think of these events as unexpected deposits of faith, sort of like the COVID19 stimulus checks many of us received. All of a sudden, we get a deposit into our bank of faith that we were not expecting. I refer to these deposits of faith as epiphanies or revelations that occur at separate distinct times that are part of God's design for our individual exclusive faith journey. I believe each of us has a faith journey specifically designed in time and sequence to deliver deposits of faith to carry us through our journey. Much like an infant is eventually nurtured from liquids to more solid food, we are nurtured in our faith, from faith to faith as scripture says. Early in my faith journey I was taught to reject any experience that is not recorded in scripture. All I can say is that if I subscribed to that philosophy, none of what follows would have happened and I believe my faith would have eventually gone cold, stale and inactive. Let me quote from the character Andy Dufresne in the movie Shawshank Redemption, "Get busy living or get busy dying". I believe that to be true with regard to our faith. What follows is a description of some of the key events of my faith journey. I hope they are helpful.

I previously referred to an episode in my faith journey that was probably the first type of event, epiphany or revelation that I am referring to in this chapter. Without recounting the details of the event, let me simply say that what occurred in me at that non-denominational service on that business weekend, was something that I had never before experienced. It was a cathartic drain of pent-up emotion that had been a part of me my whole adult life up to that point. I cannot tell you what the source of those feelings were or when I first noticed them. All I can remember is that starting sometime in my college days, I carried deep in my soul an anger that never quite abated. I do not know even exactly what I was angry about, but this slow burn of emotion was there all the time, just below the surface, ready to show itself when the pressures of life caused it to spill out. From that day, that moment at that service that anger went away. I am not claiming that I have never been angry since that day. What I am declaring is that constant state of heart that resides deep inside, that must be constrained, ignored or temporarily dealt with in some fashion – it was gone! Permanently, never to return! Something that exists unseen, known to no one but me. How? Who could know of something like that? If anyone ever suspected I was dealing with something like that, it was never mentioned to me by anyone. Only someone greater than me, that knows me better than myself. Someone who cares enough about me, to fix me, has the ability to do so, and then fixes that condition without my even asking. In that moment God became real to me. No one had to convince me that He cared for me more than I cared for myself. Some call it miraculous. I call it the evidence of things unseen. At that moment faith became real to me.

At that point, my faith journey was launched. Initially belonging to a Baptist church, I had the opportunity to learn much. I attended dozens of bible classes that were both formal and informal instruction. Through that study I learned that the form and function of evangelical faith varied with the denomination. Different forms of worship and prayer existed to coincide with different interpretations of scripture's meaning and its current relevance. However, I became very defensive and uncomfortable whenever I was around those who believed differently than I did. The immaturity of my faith could not handle a reasonable argument of faith that was different from my own without feeling threatened or inferior in some way. Often one's defense mechanism is to criticize those who believe differently, and I was often quick to do just that. My particular issue was with Pentecostal evangelicals who worshipped differently and believed that the spiritual gifts described in scripture were still relevant. Pentecostals were vibrant and free to express themselves in worship. They would do outrageous things like raise their hands, clap and shout while singing in church which I found irreverent and pretentious. I felt those old feelings of anger and anxiety begin to build deep inside me whenever I was around that type of believer. That all changed in me in a moment one Saturday morning in a men's retreat in the beautiful rolling hills of Louden County, VA. A couple of friends of mine arrived at my house on a Thursday afternoon and literally kidnapped me to go on a four-day men's retreat. They did not gag and bind me, they just made all the arrangements, including packing an overnight bag for me and shamed me into going with them. Every excuse I offered not to go had been taken care of and I felt like I would look foolish and afraid if I did not go with them. Once a Baptist preacher told me that pride will take us a long way. That afternoon I jumped into the car, after all my pride was at stake!

Upon arrival all watches were turned in to the registration desk to be returned on Sunday afternoon and we were instructed to make no contact with the outside world for the entire weekend. (There were no public phones, and this was before cell phones were readily available.) Private rooms were provided, and all meals were literally served to the participants; we had nothing to do but be served and receive what the weekend offered. To be honest, during the first few days there was not anything taught or shared that was new to me and I was feeling at that point that this was a colossal waste of time. I believe it was the second evening a paper bag was waiting for me in my room. It was filled with personal notes from mostly people I did not know that said they were praying and fasting for me that weekend. That struck me. The next morning after breakfast we had an outdoor lecture in a group of about 20 men sitting in a semi-circle around a wooden cross. We took turns symbolically nailing our stresses and anxieties (recorded on a small piece of paper) to the cross, each taking a turn with a nail and a shared hammer. Each guy would go up to the cross .... (Whack!) ..... and return to his seat. I think I was stressing about work, family, kids .... the usual stuff. After all the symbolic sins (stresses) had been nailed to the cross, we remained seated, and I noticed out of the corner of my eye that suddenly the guys on the end of the semi-circle began to weep and some began to hug one another. I sat there as this wave started making its way around the semi-circle towards me. Right before it passed me, I remember thinking "Oh, no! Here it comes!" And I closed my eyes! As it passed, I began to weep. Slow at first but weeping quickly grew into sobbing. No one spoke to me, no one hugged me or touched me. Just as years ago at that Sunday service on the business weekend I cried out all the anxiety that had been built in the recesses of my heart without really knowing it. When I stopped crying, I felt drained, peaceful, and somehow relieved. I had no idea what had happened until later that same day when we gathered at a lakeside to sing some hymns. For the first time in my life, I found myself free to worship as never before, my arms uplifted, clapping, and hopping around in pure freedom and joy of worshipping God! What I did not realize was that the judgement and critical spirit I previously had towards others who were free to worship God in that way was blocking me from enjoying the same experience. That bitterness was purged from me without even asking for it. Once again God knew my issue before I even recognized it myself and decided to rid me of it just like many years before at that Sunday service. That moment freed me to move into a full Pentecostal experience of my faith. That ability to praise and worship God has never left me from that day. My faith had changed; I had moved from faith to faith.

Both of the previous experiences occurred in a church community. Each event was associated with a different denomination, but both were evangelical churches. Each church had doctrinal positions in that community to explain my experience. Each had their own church vernacular for the particular event. The first event occurred when my church community was Baptist, the second when my church community was Assembly of God. The first was a non-Pentecostal church, the second was a Pentecostal church. The first experience was described by both churches as "being saved". The second event was described as the "baptism of the Holy Spirit" which is accepted in the Pentecostal church (my second church) but not the non-Pentecostal church (my first church). I will deal with the doctrines of faith in a later chapter. However, neither of these experiences happened in the prescribed manner or order held by each church's doctrinal positions. In other words, both churches agreed with my experiences, but they did not agree with the manner or sequence in which my experiences occurred. In one instance, I had a pastor tell me my experience was invalid because the sequence was out of order. If you are confused, you should be, I certainly was at times. My point is simply God works in each of our lives in a manner and a custom in which fits us best. Doctrine is good. Denominational customs are helpful. But these are all methods for men to try to explain what God is doing in an individual's life. They are helpful and necessary, but I believe they do not constrain God in how He wants to meet you or me. I further believe God meets us right where we are.

My faith journey continued in the Pentecostal community and my faith continued to grow. On Father's Day June 18, 1995 at the Brownsville Assembly of God Church in Pensacola, Florida a revival movement started. If you are not familiar with this event, feel free to research the background of it and others like it. They are well documented. Such events have occurred sporadically in the history of the church and are sometimes referred to as "awakenings", all to indicate something is happening with a particular community of faith outside its normal routine. In this case, the "Brownsville Revival" continued for about five years. I had the opportunity to visit the revival after it had been active for several years. I would characterize the services as highly charged and lengthy, including a time of worship, preaching and personal ministry time for praying with attendees. People waited in long lines for admission to the services. People arrived early and often lingered long after the service was over. People were in no hurry to leave because the atmosphere was different from any I had ever experienced before in church. A pastor from Missouri who was struggling with a church crisis visited the "Brownsville Revival" in 1996. What resulted upon his return to his church was a similar experience that became known as the "Smithton Outpouring". His church of 150 members ended up hosting a three-year revival (awakening) that experienced approximately 250,000 visitors. I also had an opportunity to visit that "outpouring". I found the environment similar to "Brownsville" with the services tailored to that community.

I am not a person given to seek sensationalism or experiences for experience's sake. Any spiritual experience I have ever had was not intentionally sought out or even discussed in a public way up until this writing. My experiences in these "revival" services were very personal and not planned in any way. The simplest way to describe my reaction while attending these services was that there was a feeling of weight beginning on the back of my shoulders, like someone leaning on my back. This weight would continue to get heavier until I would first kneel and then eventually lie prostrate on the floor. While in this position, I felt a presence of love deep within me that was usually followed with edifying thoughts, like someone was encouraging me. The overwhelming feeling that I will never forget is that I just wanted to linger in that moment, I was in no hurry to leave it. The first time this happened I was embarrassed and thought I would be a disturbance to others. Quite the opposite happened. No one even noticed. Nothing was said to me or as far as I know about me. I was very relieved by that fact, and it reinforced the personal aspect of it to me. I have had many similar experiences since that time. Usually, it is a heaviness that I will feel on my hands, arms, or shoulders. It always occurs in a service during times of worship, not when someone is speaking or teaching. It is always very personal and private.

So, what is the purpose of all this and why in the world would I want to tell anyone about such things? For many years, I did not. I was not sure how or why I would even want to bring up the subject. But I am in a different season of my life and my faith now. I now believe this experience is an extension of my faith journey, moving "faith to faith". I want people to know God is more involved in our lives then we dare to think. I believe we are able, and it is God's desire for each of us to have an intimate personal encounter with Him, now in this time, in this place. It is not a privilege reserved only for the clergy or the gifted preacher or minister only. Yes, I believe there are special anointed leaders in every faith, like the Pope and other denominational leaders. Those are gifted individuals appointed for a certain task and responsibility. I am talking about the rest of us, the common folk, the ones that sit in the pews every Sunday. I believe most of us do not even attempt to experience God in the manner and dimension that He not only wants for us but covets for us. Why else would God heal and change us when we are not even seeking Him to do so? I think it begins with a realization that there is an evolution required by our faith that moves us from just learning about God to an experience with God. If we are still in the same place and custom of faith that we were as children, I do not think it is bad or a condemnation. I think it is a shame because we are missing so much. We need to change our minds about God and take a step of faith. Then the journey begins "faith to faith".

CHAPTER 7
Certainties of Faith

As mentioned before, after my epiphany on that Sunday morning in a non-denominational service, I began my faith journey at my friend's Baptist church. I remember attending my first service at this church, excited in anticipation of what was in store with this new step of faith. Even though my previous experiences in a Baptist church were not good, something had changed in me, and I was looking forward to this new experience. I still had no idea why these changes had occurred in my life, only that they had. I felt peaceful and hopeful for no apparent reason, even though I was still dealing with the same domestic and financial challenges. I was quite surprised when the pastor of this Baptist church showed up at my door a week later. Unknown to me at the time, it was customary for him to come by the homes of those who had visited his church. By chance he caught me at home by myself and I was happy to spill out all the details of the recent changes that had occurred in my spiritual life. No sooner did I finish my account when he proclaimed, "You got saved!" I was not sure if I had ever heard that expression before but nevertheless it sounded like it was a nice thing to have experienced. He went on to explain the simple plan of redemption through faith in Christ, and therefore being spared an eternal life of judgement in hell. Of course, I was familiar with all those terms through my Catholic experience but at no time had I thought of myself as one on track for eternal judgement in hell. I remember thinking "Whew! Glad I missed that!". Looking back at the moment I am surprised my reaction was so cavalier. I think it was because I respected this young pastor's time and opinion, and I was so open to a change in my thinking about faith and my attitude towards God. I knew my faith had pretty much run its course under its current construct and I thought it was time to make some changes to it. I became like a sponge absorbing all the details of this new denominational experience, not challenging anything but accepting what was taught as being time-tested and with no reason to doubt its truth, accuracy, or effectiveness. I readily accepted all the Baptist denominational doctrines and became an eager defender of the faith.

I believe most people have the same experience over time as knowledge, understanding and experience in one's faith grows, perspectives begin to change. Meacham writes "In writing the gospels, and then in formulating church doctrine in the second, third, and fourth centuries, Jesus's followers reacted to his failure to return by reinterpreting their theological views in light of their historical experience. If the kind of kingdom they had so long expected was not at hand, then Jesus's life, death and resurrection must have meant something different. The Christ they looked for in the beginning was not the Christ they had come to know. His kingdom was not literally arriving, but he had, they came to believe, created something new: the church, the sacraments, the promise of salvation at the last day – whenever that might be."[2] None of us are confronted with the challenges that were confronted by Christ's apostles in formulating the doctrines of the faith. Currently our

---

[2] The Hope of Glory: Reflections on the Last Words of Jesus from the Cross by John Meacham; p.23, Convergent Books, 2020.

challenge is separating the doctrines of our particular brand of faith versus what should instead be characterized as dogma. Doctrine is, of course, the body of principles or positions of a particular system of belief. Dogma are principles or beliefs put forth as authoritative without adequate grounds. This is where it gets fuzzy. Who or what one holds as an adequate ground of authority varies with the denomination of the church. In other words, who or what authority that assures an individual what to accept as a principle of faith varies. Additionally, the effectiveness of that authority may wane based on one's experience in that faith. For instance, a person that is a recent convert to Catholicism will most likely willingly accept any decree from the Pope because he is the commonly accepted authority. However, someone who has been a Catholic all his or her life may be skeptical of Papal decrees based on his or her experience in the faith over that issue. Similar to the way in which the apostles' positions of belief held by their faith changed with their experience of that faith.

I have alluded to the way in which some of my doctrinal positions changed as my faith changed with my experiences. Even through these changes, I still agree with most of the common doctrines held by the evangelical communities. However, several years ago it became obvious to me that most discussions on the topic of hell used the text on "Abraham's bosom" found in Luke 16:22ff. Clearly this text cannot be taken literally, consequently it must be a metaphor. The consistent reference to this text as literal when teaching or preaching on the subject of hell left me with many questions, which prompted me to do some study. There has been extensive discussion and study on this topic. I recommend Rob Bell's treatment in his book "Love Wins" as being an exhaustive scriptural study on hell. Carlton Pearson's discussion on hell in his book "The Gospel of Inclusion" is also a good discussion to read. My point is this, in my opinion the topic of hell falls in the category of "dogma" rather than "doctrine". That is, there is certainly enough documented study on the subject and such a diversity in opinion that I would have to say that there is some doubt with regard to which category the topic of "hell" falls within - doctrine or dogma. Unfortunately, hell is a doctrine that is central to the mission and function of the evangelical community. Specifically, the motivation to "evangelize" is to save people from hell. It is a good motive, pure in its intent. What causes a problem is the emphasis placed on the subject of hell given the uncertainty of the doctrine.

It is hard to imagine the peer pressure that exists within some denominational churches unless you are involved in the individual church planning and the execution of those plans. Also, in my experience, those churches that emphasize evangelism the most are those most concerned with the statistics of church growth in attendance and offerings. My involvement as a lay teacher and minister in several churches required the weekly recording of attendance, which was then discussed in great detail at weekly meetings. Routine planning sessions were held strategizing how to set and attain increased attendance goals. This was all done in the name of "evangelism". I attended several services at Thomas Roads Baptist Church in Lynchburg, VA when Jerry Falwell, Sr. was pastor. I remember once his account of being approached by a Pentecostal pastor advocating that Pastor Falwell's church would benefit if it were Pentecostal as well. Pastor Falwell's response was to compare attendance and offering numbers of the two churches. Falwell's numbers were much greater, resulting in the crowd's thunderous response cheering and applauding. Unfortunately, this same mentality translated when I pastored my own church. I constantly obsessed over attendance and financial statistics. In a church start up, the pressure is even more intense because there is a fine balance that must be struck between encouraging people to get involved and to invite friends to church without sounding desperate. In fact, this exact comment was made to me when I was trying to recruit a youth pastor for my church. He eventually agreed to come on staff but said he was initially hesitant because I sounded so desperate for help. Sad to say, that desperation was out of the desire to grow my church and grow the numbers. I knew having a youth pastor on staff was a critical element to make that happen. Unfortunately, my desperation to grow the church was showing through my best intentions.

Experiencing Christ through my faith has provided some of the most profound, exhilarating, joyful experiences of my life. However, during much of the time doing the ministry of my faith the experience was clouded by a sense of not measuring up and not being a successful servant of my faith. I recognize now that this was a result of my personal vulnerabilities and of trying to please my authorities in the faith, combined with an extreme dose of competitiveness. This is where the emphasis to expand the size and effectiveness of one's church or ministry through evangelism may become a little misguided. I believe every pastor or minister intends to affect people's faith in only a positive way and it is only in that intent that sometimes some co-laborers in the faith get hurt and lost along the way. Reflecting on this experience has caused me to ask myself how different would my experience have been if it were based solely on the joy in my heart from knowing Christ and not based on "saving souls" and the pressures of comparing my efforts to the success of others? I venture a guess that it would have been a much different experience.

All the above begs the question, if evangelicals should modify the emphasis on evangelism, then what are the certainties of our faith? In other words what are the things we can count on that will not change based on our interpretation of doctrine and our experiences in our faith? Let me circle back to the account I discussed in the beginning of this chapter when the young pastor declared to me "You just got saved!". Why is it, up to that point in my life, the question of my salvation was never an issue with me? I believe it is because from an early age the concept that God exists was nurtured in me so that by the time I arrived at adulthood it was never a consideration with me. I was certain there was a God and the relationship I had with Him was limited but typical and as developed as I understood it to be possible at that time. I believe this is the critical element required to initiate one's faith as described in scripture. "But without faith it is impossible to please Him (God), <u>for he who comes to God must believe that He is</u>, and that He is a rewarder of those who diligently seek Him." (Hebrews 11:6) In other words, every faith journey begins with this first step as a requirement – "must believe that He is" – believe God exists. I heard it stated once that scripture never tries to prove God's existence, God is simply quoted as "I am" – take it or leave it, believe it or not, our choice. Thanks to my Catholic beginnings I never have doubted that God exists. I may not have always lived like that knowledge had any significance to me, but I never doubted His existence. But it does not end there. Faith is initiated with believing God exists and also that "He is a rewarder of those who diligently seek Him." I believe the two statements are conditional. That is, our belief in the existence of God releases in us the understanding that if we diligently pursue that faith, we will be rewarded in some way by God. That concept was instilled in me as a child, not so much in terms of redemption from my bad self but more of an acceptance by God just as I was. I believe that is why I never believed I was in danger of condemnation to hell, until I was taught to believe that doctrine as an adult. I think the certainty of our faith begins and ends with the acceptance and belief that God exists. Everything else from that point gets mixed up with denominational interpretation of our various faith communities. You name it – salvation, grace, heaven, hell, Holy Spirit, Jesus, the second coming, gifts of the

Holy Spirit, tongues, prophecy, baptism ... the list of aspects of our faith to be debated are endless. I would be untruthful if I said that sometimes all these differences, or uncertainties if you will, of our faith were not a source of frustration, irritation, and exasperation at times. At times they have been a source of heated debate and sometimes angry disagreement. Through that process I have come to fully accept the variations of belief within the evangelical communities of faith. What I have learned to advocate is a position my first bible teacher encouraged his students to take .... "Know what you believe and believe what you know." In other words, we each need to think through these issues of faith, research them and study them. Then we will be in position to decide what we believe and accept the fact that not everyone is going to believe the same as we do. We can be certain that the uncertainties of faith will always remain!

Let me conclude this chapter by stating the certainties of my faith. I have had many wonderful experiences in my faith journey and have found that those that were the most rewarding were in times when I least expected it. One such experience was in the joy of baptizing people new to embracing Christ – children, teens, young and mature adults. There are few experiences in the faith more exhilarating than that privilege. My church's baptismal services were held at a local YMCA pool often while public swim classes were being conducted at the other end of the pool. Whole families would turn out to see their loved one being baptized, most who had never attended a service in my church until then. It was truly a celebration of faith for all those who came to be a part of the baptism and for all the others who happened to be in the vicinity of the pool at the same time.

Other joyful experiences included joining couples in marriage. I had the privilege of re-marrying one couple that had divorced years previously but had reconciled in my church. I had the joy of marrying twin sisters (at separate times). I also had the privilege of conducting the marriage of my stepdaughter to a young man whose family was Muslim. We held the ceremony in the lobby of a beautifully landscaped hotel because his family would not enter a Christian church. Also, I had the privilege of conducting one funeral, that of the gentleman I spoke about earlier that impacted my faith so dramatically while he was on his death bed. But most of all I had the privilege for seven years to have a body of believers in the same faith as mine call me pastor.

The consequences of all these wonderful experiences are to produce the two certainties of my faith. That is, God exists, and He is a rewarder of those who diligently seek Him in ways we cannot imagine. But let me share one last insight of my faith and its two certainties. I, like everyone, have had my share of pain and hurt in my life. But those certainties that God is, and He is a rewarder if we seek Him, has helped me even in the darkest times. I have come to believe that is the true reward promised in scripture as a result of seeking God. It is not a promise of material gain or being physically prosperous although both or either are certainly possible. I believe the true reward is knowing the presence of God in our lives even in our darkest moments. Those times when we ache so much that no words or any efforts to abate the pain are helpful. It is in those times that only a sense of an abiding presence of God deep inside you gets you through to the other side of the difficulties. I also believe the true reward is knowing the presence of God in intimate times of prayer and worship. It is in those moments when you feel the God of all the Universe communicating with your heart, mind, and very core of your soul. All at once you become filled with joy, love, and acceptance on a level that you have been searching for in so many ways most of your life. It is those two opposite experiences of ultimate despair and acceptance that have formed the certainties of my faith. These certainties were not formed in a classroom, or

CHAPTER 8

Integrity of Faith

~

DURING MOST OF MY FEDERAL CAREER I WAS ACTIVELY involved in my avocation of faith. Towards the latter part of my career, I was selected for a temporary senior executive position outside the Boston area. I was the acting civilian deputy to the commanding general of a 1,000-employee organization that was located in three different geographical locations, including the Boston, Philadelphia and the Washington, D.C areas. This position came with a huge executive office complete with a view of the campus and my name hand painted on the outer glass door that led into the outer office area which was occupied by my dedicated secretary. She was a charming lady who had been in her job many years and took me under her wing by managing my daily schedule, keeping me on time and generally out of trouble. One day she came into my office to ask if I would take a meeting with an employee that was not scheduled. I had worked with this individual previously and was glad to take the meeting. Who walked into my office was an extremely attractive young lady, dressed immaculately in a smart looking business suit. She proceeded to close my office door as I rose to greet her. I had known this young lady several years previously when she was working at an entry level. She evidently had grown professionally because she had a much different look and demeanor. When she greeted me with a hug my radar went up, so I asked her to sit at the conference table while I safely retreated to a distance seated behind my desk. My instincts were proven correct because as soon as the pleasantries of catching up with her career and her congratulating me for my temporary promotion, she began to tell me how awful her husband was to her and how unhappy she was in her marriage. I had previously heard a teaching that the biggest threat to one's integrity in his or her career was the privacy that is attained with authority. At that moment that day in my office I realized I was in total control of my schedule, and I was in the position to exploit this young lady's vulnerability should I choose to do so. Instead, I chose to refer her to some marriage counseling resources of which I was aware and wished her the best. That was the end of the issue and our paths never crossed again. I believe my act of integrity that day was not any different than those made by countless officials, authorities, ministers, husbands, wives, and single people every day. Integrity can be taught, learned, and lived in a completely secular manner every day. It is the default position of our nature. But integrity of faith is different and operates on a different level if you will. It is one of those instances when the natural becomes blended with a supernatural conduct of living. Let me begin my explanation of what I am referring to as our integrity of faith by quoting King David from one of his writings (Psalms 41:12). "You uphold me in my integrity and set me before Your (God's) face forever." I guess we would all behave differently if we thought our actions were displayed on the wide screen before God twenty-four/ seven. But this is the accountability David is suggesting that he has of his own integrity. If you have read the account of David's life you know integrity was sometimes a challenge for him, but yet he is described as a "man after God's own heart" (1 Samuel 13:14). He was a man full of faith, but he struggled with his humanity at times. That is why he is one of my favorite biblical figures. But just because David felt he had this accountability for himself, does that mean we are under the same expectation? Mathew 5:28 records Jesus instructing a large crowd of followers and states the following. "But I say to you that whoever looks at a woman to lust for her has already committed adultery with her in his heart." Taken literally I think most men, including myself, would have to plead guilty, but I think the intent here is to express the notion that integrity in God's economy of faith requires an alignment of the heart attitude with our actions. That is, we are no longer to act out in ways that are in conflict with the principles of our faith that we should be holding dear in our heart. Or put a different way, integrity of faith not only addresses our actions but the motive, intent, and spirit that either accompanies or precedes our actions. This is my definition for integrity of faith. Our faith is continuous in all these areas, not exclusive to our actions. The definition of the word integrity implies the state of being complete or undivided. Therefore, I think if any division between our faith (what we believe) and our motives or attitudes and our actions would be a lack of integrity (existence of divisions)) among these elements. I think we should all agree that setting a cross (a significant symbol of our faith) on fire in front of someone's house in order to scare or intimidate the occupants of that house does not line up with the fundamentals of the Christian faith regardless of the denomination. The integrity of faith is lost among such behavior and therefore the principles of our faith are compromised. These are violations of our integrity of faith, yet we all know that actions like these by professing people of faith have been a part of our nation's history for many years.

Looking back on my experience of starting a church I realize that while having the best intentions I made many mistakes. All my previous ministry experiences were within established churches. The experience of starting a church from its beginning was unlike any previous experience. It is quite understandable that mistakes were made. What is difficult to accept is that those mistakes were based on a heart attitude that was not acceptable and where my integrity of faith was violated. One of these instances occurred when I was trying to encourage the folks in my church to be more open to demonstrating freedom in their worship experience. To me a meaningful worship experience allows the freedom to clap, shout, lift hands and even dance around if the individual feels inclined to do so in the spirit of worship. The night before this particular Sunday many of us had attended a wedding service and reception for a member of our congregation. In my morning sermon, I chose to contrast the freedom many of them had enjoyed on the dance floor the previous night with their lack of freedom of worship in church. My contention was that if they could do the first, they should be able to do the second. Not a bad illustration, but what was wrong was the attitude of my heart when I delivered the comparison. The truth of the matter is that I was frustrated and upset with a lot of the folks that Sunday morning. Instead of being a pastor thankful that many of them made the effort to get to church Sunday morning after a late evening of fun and dancing, I criticized them for their lack of consistency in their faith, or in other words I was challenging their integrity of faith. I used words like "if you could do the limbo on Saturday night, you certainly can raise your hands on Sunday morning." The truth of the matter is that the only one that Sunday morning who was in violation of his integrity of faith was me. Scripture clearly teaches that those stronger or more mature in faith must always make allowances for those less mature or weaker (less mature) in faith (i.e., 1 Corinthians 8:9-13). In this case the folks in my church had not moved in their faith to a place where they felt comfortable raising their hands or any other such expression of worship besides singing. The reality of it was that many of them had come from a more traditional style of worship including hymnals and congregational singing. What I was suggesting was an expectation on my part that they would be more mature in their faith if they worshipped more like me, which is incorrect. The measure of one's faith is not based on one's method of worship. My words were meant for an exhortation to a new worship experience, but my spirit was angry, judgmental, and hurtful to all who heard them – that was a violation of my integrity of faith. God's economy of faith consistently blends our natural experience with supernatural results. What I said in my natural course of ministering had a dramatic effect on the spirits of my church members. It was just a matter of time before most of the folks that I was mad at that day left my church and never returned. It was a hard lesson to learn, but a necessary one to move forward in faith.

I write these words at a unique time in our country, at least during my lifetime. I will discuss the relationship of faith and our country in the next part, but the topic of integrity of faith has a direct connection to some recent events that I feel is appropriate to discuss at this time. A few months ago, our nation's Capitol was besieged by a political rally that became violent as it unfolded. I have lived in the Washington D.C. area most of my adult life and being a retired civil servant, I take great interest in the events involving the city and our nation's Capitol. When the political rally held on Jan.6, 2021 turned ugly, I watched in utter horror and disbelief at the explicit news coverage. After prolonged viewing of all the various video recordings of the day's events from many angles and perspectives, I was left with an observation regarding the integrity of faith. There were several instances in which I could hear in the various videos' expressions like "God sent us!", "We are following God's will!", or "We are fighting for God's leader!". At some angles or views, a cross that was being carried in the vicinity of the violence could be seen. I am not suggesting this was a religious movement or that a significant number of folks on the mall that day were making a profession of faith in any way. But I am certain that there were a few folks there that day that felt their actions were in line with and or justified by their faith to some degree. This is hard to imagine except that all things considered the idea is not too far from the concept of burning a cross on someone's lawn in the name of God. In my opinion, for contradictions of faith like this to occur, first one would have to ignore the many scriptural references to submission to authority (i.e., Romans 13:1-3, 1 Peter 2:13-14). Causing property damage to Federal buildings, hurting law enforcement personnel physically and causing the deaths of several individuals cannot be construed in any way as submission to authority. So, the question is how does someone of faith get to a place or position that is so obviously opposed to the fundamentals of one's faith? I believe it is an issue of the integrity of one's faith versus the compartmentalization of one's faith. As discussed, integrity of faith requires there be no divisions or gaps in our faith between our faith's fundamental beliefs, the motives of our heart and our actions. They all should be continuous, like an unbroken line. Compartmentalization of our faith is when we manage our faith in isolated areas, for instance separating our motives from our actions. One of my prime examples is to say "Well God knows my heart" to excuse some action I want to take that I know does not quite square up with my faith. In such an example, I will use my rational mind to put this set of circumstances in its own compartment and separate it from my faith in general. Things like cheating on our income taxes or telling "white" lies. I remember as a child my mother telling me to give my teacher an excuse for my absence at a school function that was not true. When I challenged her on it, she told me "white lies" were acceptable. I guess I continued with the practice as an adult, but this really is an oversimplification of the main issue. The problem is that in my experience, if one becomes comfortable in these types of oversimplifications of our faith, it becomes easier to compromise on issues with larger moral, relational, and sometimes legal implications. Early in my faith journey I was associated with a youth pastor from Alabama. He was young but wise far beyond his years. He would often say in his southern drawl "It's always right to do right!". He would always get a laugh every time he said it, but over the years I have learned to appreciate the wisdom of that simple truth. It is always right to do right and a whole lot simpler when it comes down to it. That is integrity of faith.

PART 3
FAITH REVEALED IN A NATION

A dear member of my family has the unique job that involves the breeding of horses. She is responsible for the care of several mares as they approach the delivery time of their coveted foals. Her job sometimes involves long nights because there are no maternity wards or prenatal care centers for these horses, they simply require attention when their foal is imminent. Election day occurs during foaling season and this year my relative in her rush to vote was surprised to learn when she arrived at the poll that this was a presidential election year. I remember when my life was so full of making a living, parenting, and pursuing my avocation that I too did not pay much attention to current events or the details of the affairs of our country. There simply was not enough time in the day to research details of an election, the candidates, and their policies. Once in a while I would catch some insightful information on the evening news, but those occasions were infrequent. Usually, my selection came down to which candidate aligned best with my values of faith. It was not an extensive analysis of those issues either for it usually came down to one single issue. I believe most people and most evangelicals are similar. That is, choosing who will run our country comes down to usually one or two key issues. Those issues may vary slightly but if most evangelicals were like me, it hardly ever did. Most are too busy with work, family and covering our basic responsibilities to think about the governance of our country and the associated issues with that governance. Moreover, the issues of the day seem to be more complex not only because of the amount of detailed information available concerning dozens of issues but the unlimited perspectives and commentary that is available on each and every topic because of cable news and social media networks. As a result, we have an informational environment with alternative and sometimes competing facts and a general blurring of the truth. Truth becomes relative to one's perspective based on these blurred facts. I believe that it is in this environment that faith may play a more prominent role in the governance of our nation than ever before. I believe the faith of the people in our nation is expressed in the election of its leaders. I also believe, and will discuss in the coming chapters, that the outcome of these elections has a lot to do with previously discussed aspects of faith: the consequences, the evolution, the certainties, and the integrity of our faith. What I hope to do, in this part of the text, is to connect the outcomes of those issues of faith to our nation's present state. What I would like to bring into discussion are four faith related areas: the relevance of being "one nation under God"; the contribution of faith in the current polarization of our nation; the relationship of faith in our selection of elected officials; and the relationship between faith and the constitution. I hope you find the discussion helpful.

CHAPTER 9
One Nation Under God

~

"I pledge allegiance to the flag of the United States of America, and to the Republic for which it stands, one nation under God, indivisible with liberty and justice for all."

I CAN REMEMBER RECITING THE ABOVE PLEDGE OF ALLEGIANCE in first grade every morning when we would line up in the auditorium and recite it before we were marched off to our classroom. I can also remember in high school starting every morning standing and reciting this same pledge after the morning prayer. You can understand my surprise, when I began teaching in public high school decades later, that students had the option to stand and say the pledge of allegiance and morning prayer had been replaced with a moment of silence. In my experience, to the credit of today's students, most still willingly submit to the time-honored tradition of standing and reciting the pledge of allegiance with rare exceptions and all students respect the moment of silence, sitting quietly at their desks. But the fact of the matter is nothing stays the same, all things change. "To everything there is a season, a time for every purpose under heaven" (Ecclesiastes 3:1). Even the pledge of allegiance quoted previously has changed over time. Originally written in 1892 by Francis Bellamy as a general pledge to be used by any country, it has experienced four changes to reach its current version. The last change added the words "under God" after being proposed by President Eisenhower and approved by congress in 1954. So, someone like myself being taught as a child that we are "one nation under God" would naturally assume that people generally accepted that to be a fact. That was my general impression through my high school years. This was largely attributed to most students in my high school being from the same economic, social and racial structure. Out of approximately 360 students in my graduating class we had one non-white student. I cannot recall any students in our class that had immigrated to our country. Since those days, I have had the experience of teaching in four public high schools in two different states. In that experience I found each school to have a student body that was economically, socially and racially diverse with many students from immigrant families. Many of these immigrant families come with a wide range of faith experiences to include such faiths as Muslim, Buddhism and Hinduism. For those students to say a pledge of "one nation under God" would have a different context than mine. Certainly, we can understand how unsettling it would be for a child or young teen having to participate in a prayer if it was in conflict with his faith. Looking back, I can remember that when changes to prayer in public schools were first introduced, they were met with stiff resistance from people of faith. These changes were opposed by those who perceived them as an effort to erode our nation's values away from its Judeo-Christian roots. I now realize these changes were made to preserve the freedom of religion for all in our nation and to avoid the perception of a government preference of faith consistent with the constitution's establishment of free exercise regarding religion. This illustrates that the pledge we state during the most solemn times has been drastically misunderstood by a large segment of our nation's population, specifically in the evangelical faith communities. Early in my experience in those communities it was believed that being "one nation under God" meant that we should all believe, pray, and accept God in similar terms and in similar ways. I am not sure how much that general view still exists in those faith communities today but would not be surprised if it is still the prevailing view.

For a nation to be under God it does not require the same faith. I personally believe God is not threatened by the existence of many faiths or even the deviations within the same faith as I have chronicled in the preceding chapters of this text. I believe all expressions of faith (or religion) are man's attempt to understand the mind and heart of God, something that is way beyond our comprehension. I once heard the metaphor that our efforts of trying to understand the working and intent of God is similar to an ant that has stumbled across a picnic on a blanket and is trying to figure what it is all about and how it got there. That is something that is impossible for the ant to do. All he can try to do is benefit from and enjoy that which has been put in front of him. If we adopted that perspective, perhaps our individual communities of faith would take a different approach. That is, instead of trying to judge which faith is acceptable in the sight of God, maybe we should focus on celebrating our own faith and respecting the celebration of others in theirs. I choose Christianity. Not everyone does. I choose Pentecostal Christianity. Not everyone does. That does not make one's choice of faith any more or less valuable in the eyes of God if done with a sincere intent of heart to try to know God and earn favor in His sight. Our best and most sincere efforts to convince folks that our particular brand of faith should be preferred will fall short of our aspirations because the focus on that kind of effort is misplaced. Let me illustrate with an experience from my early days of ministry.

The Washington D.C. area during the 1980's was experiencing an intense increase in the immigrant Hispanic community. My pastor approached me about starting a Hispanic Ministry within the oversight of the church. Looking for any new ministry experience, I jumped at the opportunity. I was introduced to a couple of church members who spoke Spanish fluently and we were off and running! We routinely visited areas that were heavily populated with Hispanic immigrants. One such area was in Arlington, VA that was so dense with immigrants from Central America it was referred to as "Chirilagua" which is a municipality in El Salvador. We went door to door, often being invited into homes because the people were generally very courteous and gracious. They were exceedingly kind and open to any discussion of faith. Often, they were willing to receive any suggestion of our faith that we would make. Would you like to pray? "Si, senor!" Would you like to come to my church? "Si, senor!" Would you like to receive my faith? "Si, senor!" At first, I thought my friendly manner and articulate persuasion of faith were yielding high results. After a while I became suspicious and asked my companion why these folks were so receptive to us? He said it was because they were afraid that if they did not respond favorably, we would turn them into immigration. Of course, it made perfect sense, but in my zeal, I was completely blind to the possibility that that was the reason. When we enter the realm of faith, we are no longer on natural terms. One's faith is not activated through natural means; it requires something supernatural. One's understanding cannot change, one's heart cannot open, one's mind cannot be renewed without God. Supernatural and natural intersect and the evidence that is manifested is faith. It really does not matter how well-intentioned a minister of the faith is. I do not think people can be won over to faith or recruited into a particular faith community in any meaningful way through our fervor, our campaigns, or our polished presentations. Any true faith activity is the result of something that is "born from above" (John 3:3). It is done by God, for God. Sometimes we are the target of God's intent, sometimes we are fortunate enough to be in the vicinity when He works in someone's life. All our efforts are honorable, but we give those efforts much more credit than they deserve. I think our efforts would be better spent honoring each other's faith, striving to be "one nation under God indivisible, with liberty and justice for all." Moreover, I believe our nation is in desperate need for such an initiative, to begin within our communities of faith.

Putting all the history aside, when we cover our heart with our hand and voice our allegiance to our flag, we are indirectly pledging our loyalty to a nation, which in our case is a republic. Being a republic means having a government with a chief of state who is not a monarch (king or queen). But the pledge goes on to state that our republic has the specific attributes, first "being under God", then united (without division) and it is operating under the presumption everyone within our nation is treated freely (with liberty) and fairly (with justice). I would suggest that the last three attributes (united, free, and fair) cannot be achieved without the first "being under God". It is my opinion that during the last few years it has become evident to the entire world that we are a nation that is greatly divided and a nation that is struggling with administering liberty and justice for all. We are a divided nation in our political approach to our governance. We are a nation that struggles with the injustice being served in the prosecution of crimes against Black and Asian members of our nation. And it is clear to all that because of these divisions and injustices in our nation, there is a resulting loss of liberty for many in our nation. I think the heart of the problem begins with being "one nation under God." I think it is safe to say that this is an endeavor that cannot and will not be easily achieved. But if it can be achieved the effort must begin with our communities of faith. One of the biggest challenges in our nation today is the great racial division that exists in many elements of our society. This includes our communities of faith. I have heard it said that one of our countries most segregated times each week is on Sunday morning. Let me illustrate my point through another experience from my days of ministry.

I was in a season without church membership preparing to launch my own church when I was invited to be part of a local black congregation. The senior pastor was a neighbor of mine and we had become friends. When he learned of my desire to start a church, he offered his help and support. He was currently pastoring a thriving church of several hundred members, one that he had started many years earlier. His church had grown to such an extent that they were in the middle of constructing their own church facility and there was an excitement and unity in the membership that I had not experienced for many years. His invitation was for me to be a part of his ministry for a season to learn from his experience and when the time was right, he would support the launching of my church. To have a pastor of an established church in the community offer that kind of support was unmatched. I had been in the local area almost 20 years by that time. I had taught classes, run various ministries, served in church leadership, and worked in various administrative capacities in three established churches ranging in size from a few hundred to a thousand members or more. I did so willingly, not expecting anything in return except the joy and satisfaction in doing these various works. These churches were all predominately white including the congregations, senior pastors, and staff. In all three churches the senior pastors were well aware of my preparations for future ministering by proctoring exams for my graduate studies. So, I found it very curious that the only offer of support I received when beginning my church was from a black pastor whose church I had never visited before. He had walked the path that I was about to follow, and he wanted to help by sharing his knowledge in that experience with me. That was very meaningful to me at the time, but even more so now.

The next six months were a test of my perseverance and endurance in my faith. My involvement in this black congregation was varied in responsibility but comprehensive in its involvement. My primary teaching responsibilities were in the church's locally hosted bible college program offered through an extension program of a black university in North Carolina. I taught two courses two nights a week for two semesters. In addition, I had opportunities to minister in retreats for men and couples at various times. Besides services on Friday evenings and Sunday afternoons, I was asked to participate in the Saturday morning men's group, Sunday morning conference calls with black pastors along the east coast, and intercessory prayer on Sunday evenings. I was totally immersed in that black church community and was only one of two white males in a congregation of several hundred black men. I made many close relationships, and it was an experience that I will never forget.

The men's accountability group was held every Saturday morning at 6:30. It was an informal setting because the time and the size of the group of about twenty to twenty-five men made it more intimate than the larger church service on Sunday. Often it was a time for us to discuss all the frustrations of the week in an open exchange with anyone who wanted to participate. There was a trust and comfort among the men that created a great liberty to discuss whatever was troubling or vexing their faith, relationships or anything else. There were no guidelines, bullet points, or prearranged topics to be discussed. It was a time that most of the men looked forward to each week. One morning the discussion turned to the racial tensions and frustrations some of the men were having at work. The discussion went on for some time with a lot of generalities concerning their struggle with "the white man". That phrase was used repeatedly and often it had a negative connotation. We were sitting in a circle, and I was the only white man present. At first, I thought that some of them were perhaps directing their comments at me for some purpose of discussion. But I soon realized that was not the case. I believe I had become such a routine part of the group that they no longer saw me as white. I was viewed as part of the group regardless of my skin color. At the time I was flattered by the thought that I had grown so close to these men that race was not an issue. That was much like my college experience many years earlier when my college class was the first to have black students. Out of a class of approximately 300 students we had 5 black students, one of whom was in the same major as I was, engineering. We became close over the four years of lectures and labs. I never saw him as black; he was just a fellow engineering student.

I held both these experiences in my heart over the years as proof to myself that I was not racially biased, and I still believe that to be true to this day. However, I now realize that view is not enough. By not seeing someone for who they really are, we are not seeing them at all. In other words, I am implying I have no great interest in the specifics of their distinction from me and am dismissing their experience as having no relevance or value to me. What it amounts to is a superficial relationship, not one interested in taking that relationship deeper or making it more personal. But here is the main point, I believe that each side is similar. In my experience I felt there was no great interest from my black brothers to get to know me, just as I made no effort to get to know them. What an awful indictment to have about each other as brothers in the faith. What is worse, I now realize I carried that same perspective through all my years of ministry and in particular my seven years of pastoring. Once again, let me repeat I do not believe I am or have ever been a racist. I just was not interested in "seeing" or knowing the context of the racial struggle in our country. I was content as a pastor to not be racially biased, but I had no interest in getting to really know any people of color in more than a superficial way. That began to change for me after the murder of George Floyd. I believe that is when our nation began to have a similar revelation. Many, many people were moved to finally "see" a black man's plight. Subsequently I have come to believe that the racial problem we have in our nation is a spiritual problem. That is, I was deeply involved in the activities of a black community of faith to the extent that I had many friends, but it never went beyond superficial relationships. I knew nothing about their personal lives or point of view and they made no effort to know mine. We called each other brother, but in truth we were little more than acquaintances. How can this exist in a community of faith? I believe it is because most communities of faith have superficial relationships with God. In my experience evangelical churches emphasize service, formalities, and knowledge at the sacrifice of experiencing God in any way but a superficial manner. No number of reparations will heal the hole being carried in the souls of generation after generation of people who have "not been seen." It will take a spiritual healing that must begin with the communities of faith. I believe communities of faith must pursue those intersections of the natural with the supernatural which are those encounters that will produce a faith free from superficiality, a faith that embraces the power of God to allow the "unseen" to be "seen" by both sides of the racial divide. How we go about such a healing will be discussed in the next part of this text.

In conclusion to this chapter let me say that we cannot begin to become "one nation under God" until the communities of faith become united as one under God. In the discussion of this chapter two examples of closing divisions in communities of faith were given. One, the acceptance of other faiths both in and out of

CHAPTER 10
The Polarization of Faith

⟿

EVEN THOUGH I LIVED IN THE WASHINGTON D.C. AREA MOST OF my adult life, the closest I have physically been to a standing president was when Jimmy Carter walked down Pennsylvania Avenue after taking the oath of office. That same day I then walked down to the grounds outside the Capitol to watch Gerald Ford depart via presidential helicopter. It was the only time I ever personally witnessed the transition of power in our nation from one president to his successor. This tradition, considered by many as the bedrock of our democracy, has been treated as an almost sacred event in the sense that it has been handled with respect, dignity and in the highest regard to ensure the preservation of the process. All that changed in the year 2021 as a result of two catastrophic events. The first was a worldwide pandemic, the second a misguided political rally which nearly disrupted the constitutional process transitioning power from one duly elected president to the next. The first was initiated by viral forces from the other side of the world, the second resulted from political forces unleashed from within our own political borders. The first resulted in a much more subdued celebration of a new president, absent overwhelming crowds and endless inaugural balls. The second almost caused our democratic process to break. The impact of the virus had no substantial impact on the transfer of power except that there was less pomp and circumstance during the transition. The second almost broke a constitutional process that has operated effectively for over 200 years. We will eventually have all the safeguards and medical protections in place through vaccines and changes to our lifestyle so that the risk of a recurrence of this pandemic will be minimal. However, I do not have the same confidence that the risk to our constitutional processes of governance has been eliminated.

I have spent most of my adult life either in civil service or in service to my faith. Both are critical elements of my life experience that I hold in high regard. That is why I find it particularly vexing that we are now witnessing the politicizing of faith communities and its effect on the governance of our nation. As I have laid out in previous chapters, our faith journey as experienced in our various communities of faith affect the growth, maturity and/or perspectives of our faith. The political process in our country has capitalized on these various perspectives of faith communities to attract their support. This process has caused "polarization" and has been employed quite effectively. I am not a political scientist, analyst or a politician. I rely on other professionals in this arena to explain these concepts. But let us start with a simple definition of "polarization" from Merriam-Webster's dictionary as "a division into two sharply distinct groups." Ezra Kline states polarization is when opinions are changed to cluster around two choices with no middle ground. Kline goes on to state that issue-based polarization leads to political-identity polarization.[3] Piecing together Webster's definition with Kline's comments we have a description of our present-day political environment. That is, if we have a population sharply divided over an issue and that issue is introduced into a political context the result will be a sharp division into two political

---

[3] Why We're Polarized by Ezra Kline; p, 32, Avid Reader Press, 2020

groups. Kline later states "In 2014, Pew reported that the single largest religious group in the Republican coalition was evangelical Protestants." Kline goes on to discuss how values change with changes in demographics and quotes Steven Levitsky and Daniel Ziblatt in *How Democracies Die,* "the two parties are now divided over race and religion – two deeply polarizing issues that tend to generate greater intolerance and hostility than traditional policy issues such as taxes and government spending." Kline goes on to amend that statement slightly: "the parties are dividing over fundamental *identities* that tend to generate intolerance and hostility, and the issue conflicts are just one expression of that division."[4] I think Kline's point is subtle but significant. At the risk of "getting over my skis" a little bit, meaning I am way out of my field of expertise, let me add my two cents worth. Our identity is more than a preference. It is how we align ourselves in a distinctive way with those who are like-minded. My identity represents who I am and what I stand for as an individual but also those with whom I stand, those who believe as I do under some condition or circumstance. When my wife and I were traveling in Europe recently we were easily identified as "Americans". We immediately understood that to mean that we were from the USA and we were proud to admit it because it was part of our identity. Political identity is more than a preference; I believe it is an alignment with others in an emotional attachment that one is willing to defend. Kline later goes on to comment that changing one's identity is a psychologically and socially brutal process. Kline goes on to refer to a "identity-protective cognition theory" held by Kahan that states that individuals subconsciously resist factual information that threatens their defining values.[5] All this sounds incredibly far-fetched to a novice like me until I turn on the nightly

---

[4] Ibid, P.38
[5] Ibid, P.96

news and hear the latest conspiracy theory being espoused by some elected official being embraced by people of faith. All of a sudden this begins to make sense. When one political party describes any proposed legislation by the opposite party as socialism, they are not assigning a new governing philosophy to that party, they are simply appealing to the faith-based communities that are hostile towards any reference to socialism. Most non-political evangelicals consider socialism to be anti-Christian at best or godless in the extreme. Either way the concept evokes fear of losing our ability to practice our faith in the form and fashion that we believe very strongly is our constitutional right. This method of persuasion is very subtle, very manipulative, and highly effective. In my opinion, political polarization is the fundamental reason evangelical faith communities whole-heartedly support candidates that represent a preferred political position but at the same time contradict that communities' values of faith with regard to their conduct, character and demeanor. In so doing, one's integrity of faith is sacrificed, one's certainties of faith are compromised and the consequences of one's faith becomes obscured. This point is plainly described by Kristen Kobes Du Mez with regard to the turning of support to Donald Trump by evangelical churches during the presidential nomination process. Du Mez writes "But as evangelical support for Trump proved to be more than a passing fancy, evangelical leaders confronted the limits of their own influence. This was true on a national level, with the old guard discovering that their endorsements of Rubio or Cruz didn't seem to be quelling the surge of support, and on the local level, as pastors realized their limits of their power even within their own congregations. "It's the most amazing thing I've ever seen," wrote evangelical activist Randy Brinson. "It's like this total reversal of the shepherd and the flock," with congregants threatening to leave their churches if their pastors opposed Trump."[6] Du Mez also writes "As the election neared, the evangelical vote for Trump seemed secure. In fact, the more unconventional, bombastic, and offensive he became, the more evangelicals seemed to rally to his side."[7] Du Mez also notes the lack of Trump support from some evangelical leaders in writing "Some evangelicals despaired of support for Trump within their own ranks. Evangelical's love for Trump was "a disgrace", Russell Moore maintained, "a scandal to the gospel of Jesus Christ and to the integrity of our witness." Jon Piper, too, parted ways with many of his conservative brethren in refusing to endorse Trump. Ed Stetzer made a last-ditch attempt to dissuade his fellow evangelicals from" selling their souls" by voting for Trump."[8] All this illustrates the effect polarization has had on the evangelical community, demonstrated in our most recent presidential elections and which continues to be acted out across the political landscape of our country. While I find this frustrating and upsetting, I understand this conflict between faith and politics. Let me walk you through my evolution of faith in this area to clarify my position.

As mentioned before, I have been a single-issue voter most of my adult life. That single issue was that of being anti-abortion or pro-life. It made my political decisions easy. Every election I would rationalize that one political party was pro-life, the other was pro-choice, as defined by their party's political platforms every four years. I reasoned that my faith constrained my choice. It also relieved me of the worry of spending any additional time thinking about a complex and at times very confusing political process. I simply did not have the time to waste and felt vindicated in my choice, year after year. Whenever I had doubts about a particular

---

[6] Jesus and John Wayne, How White Evangelicals Corrupted a Faith and Fractured a Nation by Kristen Kobes Du Mez ; P. 255, Liveright Publishing Corp., 2020

[7] Ibid, P.263

[8] Ibid, P.265

candidate for whom I was about to vote, I always reasoned that my faith compelled me to make the choice that favored my one issue. I have had many conversations with evangelical friends and family members over this issue. While often it is not verbalized, I am usually left with the impression that they are in the same dilemma of being constrained in their vote over this same one issue. I still am personally against abortion, but I have come to a place in my faith that I believe we should not support the passing of any law that makes a moral decision for someone. For instance, I believe all states have strict laws against drunk driving. Consequently, there are strict definitions with regard to levels of blood alcohol that define those instances when someone is driving drunk. Those levels are quantifiable and verifiable through accurate testing. Therefore, when someone makes the moral decision to drive drunk, they can be held accountable for any consequences of that conduct under law. They are not arrested for making the moral decision as to whether or not it is ok to drive while intoxicated, they are being arrested for exceeding the allowed blood alcohol level while driving. However, both at the beginning and the end of life, definitions become more abstract. Life's inception can be clouded by all sorts of circumstances. Rape, incest, and birth defects for example are issues that often enter into the process, not to mention the many possible complications that often arise during the birth of a child. Life's end also includes complex moral issues such as capital punishment, euthanasia, DNR (Do Not Resuscitate) orders and living wills (when considering termination of life prematurely). Not all people come to the same conclusion concerning the morality of these issues based on many factors, one of which is the individual's faith. Therefore, having quantifiable measured thresholds over such a range of moral issues is not reasonable even if it were possible to do so. Ultimately the decision depends on one's view of life, when it starts and when it should end. In other words, any law punishing someone for having an abortion is punishing them for the decision to have an abortion regardless of that person's moral position on the issue. The law is making a moral decision for them. I was much more adamant over these issues when I was younger. Life's experiences have a way of softening our view of the world. My mother was approaching her ninetieth birthday when she was hospitalized with failing kidneys. The doctor said we could extend her life an indeterminate amount of time by putting her on a dialysis machine. He also said it was an extremely invasive procedure and it would not be a comfortable living arrangement for her to be tethered to a machine and accommodating the tubes required to keep her kidneys functioning. I knew my mother was looking forward to her ninetieth birthday but I also knew in my heart she would never have forgiven me for putting her through that kind of misery to live. I declined the intervention. Many would probably agree with the decision as I am sure some would disagree. I never thought I would agree to a decision like that until faced with the circumstance. This kind of experience softened my view towards abortion but was not the only factor that changed my view. Let me explain.

Early in my career I was having a discussion with an office mate about the moral arguments of abortion. After a time, the discussion became quite heated with me insisting in a loud voice that the object of the abortion was not merely a fetus, but it was a baby starting at conception! He quickly responded with as much emotion and just as loudly "Yes, but it is not viable until many weeks after conception!". I suddenly realized we agreed that there was a life involved, we just disagreed when that life technically started. In other words, we had a different moral interpretation of the boundaries of life. Moreover, I realized I had no convincing argument to offer that would convince my coworker to move the definition of his boundary as to where life begins. Any reference

I made as to what the bible implied would have no relevance to him because he was not of the same faith community as I was. To be clear there is no biblical position on abortion. The bible only implies that life begins at some point in the womb through several references (Jeremiah 1:5, Psalm 139:13-16 for example). That experience did not change my position on abortion, but it did make me more aware of how to approach the subject with members of different faith communities.

Over the course of time, I participated in several "March for Life" demonstrations. I generally had no hesitation taking a public stand for my faith, but I do recall during those marches that I would cringe when I saw pictures of aborted fetuses being carried by some participants. I never thought that approach would do anything but repulse anyone who saw it, but I never voiced my displeasure to anyone. It was not until I pastored that my view towards abortion began to soften. It was on the occasion of visiting a couple that attended my church when the wife began sharing her struggle with forgiving herself for having had an abortion many years prior to her marriage and many years before joining any faith community. She described her agony whenever she saw one of the posters of an aborted fetus being carried in a pro-life demonstration. I then began for the first time to get a sense of the amount of hurt and pain that some women go through before and after an abortion. I began to realize that before boldly declaring something is wrong, one should consider all the various implications of that declaration to the audience that is listening. Jesus never suggested a change of behavior with a clenched fist but with opened arms. How much more should we strive to be helpful to those who have already been hurt enough by their own choices. My heart continued to change with my approach to abortion with another experience with one of my church members while pastoring. This particular lady, with her family, were members of my church in its early days. Having been recently remarried I was invited to her home because she and her new husband were already struggling in their relationship but were determined to make it work. During my visit it was revealed that this woman in her early thirties was still trying to heal from the trauma of a forced abortion she experienced as a young teenager. She was literally held down during the process and it traumatized her to the extent that she was still struggling with the effects in her third marriage. The good news is that she finally did reach some degree of healing after much persistence on her part. I think that this was the experience that caused a self-examination of a personal experience with abortion that finally changed my heart.

I was divorced from my first wife when I had a brief reconciliation with her. To be precise it was only a night of intimacy which led to a few days of talk about getting back together. Those discussions quickly ended after a few days when I concluded I had no real desire to reconcile. Too much hurt had occurred during our divorce, and I had emotionally moved on and had started dating again. After a few weeks she called me at work to tell me she thought she was pregnant. I was a non-practicing Catholic by that time and was not actively part of any faith community. Additionally, I immediately felt that I had been manipulated with an evening of intimacy to help my ex-wife out of the financial difficulties she was experiencing at the time. So, my immediate solution off the top of my head was to tell her to go get an abortion and I would pay for it. She angrily agreed but with the promise that she would legally maneuver to revoke my visitation rights with my daughter who was about four years old at the time. As it turned out, she called me a few days later to tell me she was not pregnant after all. We both were somewhat relieved and we had little communication after that phone call. It was a few months later that she died in an automobile accident. I have thought of that experience many times over the years but kept it hidden in the recesses of my heart. As a pastor, counseling these women with their pain I felt deeply hypocritical. It was only through the grace of God that I did not finance the abortion of my second child. That is a devastating thought. In God's economy, I felt as though I had already done the deed, convicted by my intent and callousness of heart. I too, along with my ex-wife, were perpetrators of abortion in spirit. I cannot fathom the hurt in her heart when I implicated her in the proposed solution through my words and financing. Facing those heart issues finally changed my position on abortion. I suspect there are many men like me, guilty in their hearts, never voicing the hurt, never resolving the pain

The hurt and the pain that accompanies this practice goes far beyond the surface and touches the deep recesses of the souls of women and men alike. It must be approached with gentle grace and without condemnation. I do not believe demonstrations, legal proceedings or politics is the solution to this issue. Current court cases exist with the intent to overturn the extent and legality of abortion in our nation. The Supreme Court is scheduled to hear one such case in a few weeks with a ruling expected next year. I believe that much of this will turn out to be political theatre. It seems likely that the Supreme Court as a worst case will revert the abortion decision back to the states, if any change does occur in our nation. It is just another issue being used as political capital to keep the faith communities "polarized" in one political camp.

The preceding experiences freed me from being a single-issue voter. Consequently, it enabled me to break through the effect of "polarization" personally in that I no longer felt morally obligated by my faith to vote for one political party. I am free to evaluate each candidate on his or her own merits. I do not have to support a candidate whose behavior compromises moral issues of integrity and honesty to support a particular political platform. Moreover, I do not have to support any candidate that shows no evidence of the characteristics of faith that I hold dear such as grace, kindness, patience and humility. To sacrifice these attributes in a potential candidate for president would be a gross violation of my faith and good common sense. Also, to do so would be to give in to the political forces driving the polarization of our faith communities. While the results of this polarization seem beneficial to some it comes at great cost to people of faith. To align ourselves with those who show no evidence of faith in their lives leads to the loss of our identity. Scripture describes the people of faith as "salt and light". Those metaphors imply we of faith provide the seasoning to the distasteful areas of life and provide the ability to see in the dark recesses of confusion. When we align ourselves with the dark and distasteful, we lose our identity. We can no longer be distinguished from the people without faith. Our faith is being offered as a sacrifice on the political altar of power and control. I contend our faith is too meaningful and valuable to be offered up so cheaply. I believe that at the heart of the polarization of our faith is an identity problem and that our faith communities are in desperate need of a new identity. This will be discussed at length in Part 4 of this text. In short, I believe faith communities can and should continue to honor and respect their distinction of beliefs, ceremony, and perspectives from other faith communities. But I believe for the most part the faith communities of today are devoid of an experiential faith. Experiential faith is at the intersection of the natural with the supernatural when the people of faith interact with the God of their faith. In that environment hearts, minds and attitudes are changed. Views take on different perspectives. Priorities change. I believe that experience of interacting with God is needed for our faith communities in order to break free from such influences as the "polarization" that exist today. I believe the future democracy of our nation depends on it.

CHAPTER 11
Electing the Elect

⌒

I BEGAN MY FEDERAL CAREER IN JANUARY 1975. AT THAT TIME, all new civil servants were required to attend a one-week orientation on Capitol Hill covering the mission and function of the federal government. I do not remember many details from what seemed to be endless talks on organizations, policies and budgets except one comment made during the week that has stuck in my mind for over fifty years. It was emphasized that the legislative process on Capitol Hill was a slow, deliberate process by design. Evidently our founding fathers realized that a cumbersome, back and forth method between the two distinctly different governing bodies of the House and the Senate was required for what was considered the essential function of debate. The initiators of our government were familiar with the concept of having opposite views on any given position or discussion, but they considered themselves statesmen. Statesmen debate issues. It is only through debate of opposing sides on an issue and sometimes protracted discourse that opinions and perspectives are changed. What a wonderful concept - elected officials methodically working through a complex issue of governance that may affect multitudes of people across our nation. In so doing they are taking time to produce effective legislation that applies to all people regardless of social standing, education and variations of faith. Compare that to our present experience on Capitol Hill. Recently I heard one senator state that a piece of legislation sponsored by the opposing political party as evil and co-authored with Satan himself. There is no doubt that this kind of vitriol existed even during the founding days of our great nation. Obviously, this is highly inflammatory religious hyperbole but it illustrates a point. This particular senator was not hesitant to use faith-related rhetoric so he must have been reasonably confident that his constituency would be comfortable with the language chosen. It is a fact that every member of congress is elected and it can be assumed that an elected official represents the people that elected him or her. Our elected officials reflect the voters that elected them. Consequently, if an official is partisan it is because the constituency that elected him or her is partisan. Large blocks of faith communities are partisan or "polarized". So how did that happen? Let us look at Du Mez's account of when this phenomenon began.

Du Mez writes "In 1980, the election widely hailed as the moment the Christian Right came into its own, evangelical voters bypassed the candidate who shared their faith tradition in favor of the one whose image and rhetoric more closely aligned with their values and aspirations. Guided by preachers like Robinson, Falwell and LaHaye, 67 percent of white evangelical voters chose Reagan over Carter; just four years earlier, Carter had received 49 percent of the evangelical vote and 56 percent of the white Baptist vote."[9] Du Mez goes on to state "From Reagan on, no Democrat would again win the majority of white evangelical support or threaten the same. Evangelical's loyalty to the Republican party would continue to strengthen, and they would use their electoral clout to help define the Republican agenda for the generation to come."[10] Competing

---

[9] Ibid, p.106
[10] Ibid, p.106

with this migration of the evangelical community to a single political party was the fact that the overall trends of Christianity have been downward. Pew Research Center's telephone survey conducted in 2018 and 2019 showed 65% of American adults were self-described as Christian, down 12% from the previous decade. In other words, the faith community has been shrinking and shows no signs of changing from any political trends being experienced currently. This trend showed its effect as recently as the Republican primaries of 2016. Carney writes "The more frequently a Republican reported going to church, the less likely he was to vote for Trump in the early primaries. Trump was weakest among those Republicans who go to church the most (32% of this group voted for him in the primaries) and did nearly twice as well (62%) among those who never go to church. Each step down in church attendance brought a step up in Trump support."[11] However by election day there seemed to be a dramatic turn. According to the Washington Post - "An analysis of the 2016 electorate completed by Pew shows that white evangelicals and white Catholics were more supportive of Trump than any other religious group. He won the latter group by 33 points and evangelicals by 61 points over Hillary Clinton. More importantly Pew's data suggests that more than half the votes for Trump received that year came from voters who fit into one of these two groups. A fifth of his support was from white Catholics. Fully a third was from white evangelical Protestants."[12]

How does such a large portion of the faith-based community change their perspective on a political candidate in such a short time from the primaries to election day? Several reasons are offered as an explanation. One explanation is that (quoting Du Mez) "evangelical elites raised the specter of "fake evangelicals" - of

---

[11] Alienated America by Timothy P. Carney, p.121

[12] "A Third of Trump's Support in 2016 Came from Evangelicals and He Hasn't Lost Them Yet" by Phillip Bump, Washington Post, dated June 5, 2020

"culture Christians" - masquerading as real evangelicals. No true, Bible-believing, family-values evangelical could vote for a man like Trump, they insisted. The pollsters were using flawed categories. In the aftermath of Trump's election, many pundits pointed to economic motivations behind support for Trump more generally, and some applied this reasoning to his white evangelical base as well (end quote)."[13] However according to Du Mez, "support for Trump was stronger among those who perceived their status to be most imperiled, those who felt whites were more discriminated against than blacks, Christians than Muslims and men than women. In short, support for Trump was strongest among white Christian men. Many evangelicals themselves claimed to have "held their noses" when they voted for Trump as the lesser of two evils. Certain "character flaws" might be overlooked in the interest of defending religious freedom and protecting the lives of the unborn... ... however, for many evangelicals, Donald Trump did not represent the betrayal of many of the values they had come to hold dear. His testosterone-fueled masculinity aligned remarkably well with that long championed by conservative evangelicals. What makes for a strong leader? A virile (white) man. And what of his vulgarity? Crudeness? Bombast? Even sexual assault? Well boys will be boys. God-given testosterone came with certain side effects, but an aggressive and even reckless masculinity was precisely what was needed when dealing with the enemy.... evangelicals hadn't betrayed their values. Donald Trump was the culmination of their half-century-long pursuit of a militant Christian masculinity. Unencumbered by traditional Christian virtue, he was a warrior in the tradition (if not the actual physical form) of Mel Gibson's William Wallace. He was a hero for God-and-country Christians in the line of Barry Goldwater, Ronald Reagan, and Oliver North, one suited for *Duck Dynasty* Americans and American Christians,

---

[13] Jesus and John Wayne by Kristen Du Mez, p.266

He was the latest and the greatest high priest of the evangelical cult of masculinity".[14]

At this point we must pause and try to digest what was just discussed. The preceding is just a sample of the analysis that has been done from these referenced works. Each of them contains a volume of opinion, data and discussion concerning recent political events and communities of faith. Even when presented with these evangelical behavior rationalizations, I cannot ignore the fact that scripture refers to people of faith as the "elect". The prophet Isaiah uses this same description when referring to Jesus as "God's elect" (Isaiah 42:1) and later refers to all of Israel as the "elect" (Isaiah 45:4). The apostle Peter refers to all Christians as the "elect" (1 Peter 1:2) as well. In Mathew's gospel the "elect" refers to those that God will gather in the latter days and goes on to imply that the "elect" have a great ability to resist deception and implies it is almost impossible to fool them (Mathew 24:24,31). Regardless of whether one considers these scriptural references as literal or symbolic, they hold people of faith in high regard. In the Old Testament, Israel represented the nation to whom God introduced Himself, a distinction of note. All Christians are put in this same high regard as a people of faith. Moreover, the context assigns a place of special note to these people not only because of their faith but they are imbued with an ability to recognize and resist deception. So, my question is simple. How can a people noted for their faith be so faithless in their selection of elected officials? In addition, how can they, being designated as a people resistant to deception because of their faith, be so easily deceived when it comes to politics? If I were asked those questions, I would have to raise my hand and say "guilty" as a former pastor. My criticism of pastors is not intended to "throw the baby out with the bath water." I love the church and have the utmost respect for all men

---

[14] Ibid, p. 267-271

and women that answer the call to pastor. Moreover, "Christ also loved the church and gave Himself for it" (Ephesians 5:25) and all those that call themselves Christian should feel similarly. But as pastors we are often conflicted in what to say and what not to say. Pastors must not sound political or partisan, but we live in fear of saying something truthful that will offend someone politically and result in them leaving the church. It is the "shepherd and flock reversal syndrome" described by Du Mez that I referred to in the previous chapter. I did my best walking that line for seven years until I could not do it anymore. I admire and edify any pastor that fights that battle year after year. Let me illustrate the struggle with another of my experiences while pastoring.

I was on my way to the airport, riding with a pastor friend. We were both pastoring in the Northern Virginia area and on our way to a denominationally sponsored conference. On the way I received a frantic call from one of my church leaders. He was a devoted and talented man. Having been trained to play trumpet, he took upon himself to learn how to play the electric keyboard and pulled together a worship team for my church. He was like a brother to me and dear to my heart because of his devotion to my church. He was calling that evening besides himself just having found some evidence that his wife was possibly being unfaithful to him. Angry and distraught, he was about to take some action that would have been destructive to his marriage and his family of five. By this time in my ministerial experience, I had experienced similar conversations with several men and these situations usually did not end well. First and foremost, you want to be compassionate and understanding but at the same time try to prevent the wounded person from doing anything that could be fatally destructive to the relationship with his or her spouse and family. That must always be balanced with not being too emphatic or overbearing lest you run the risk of losing his or her trust and he completely dismisses your relationship as his pastor. In other words, if you tick him off you probably will never see him again in your church. In this case, I had an additional emotional investment because not only was he a dear friend, but he was a critical member of my church leadership. After an extended time of listening and trying to calm him and because we were approaching the airport I knew I had to make a choice, either leave him to his own devices for the immediate time or be very direct with him and risk our relationship. I chose the latter, directing him very emphatically as to what he should do as a next step and what he should absolutely not do. Fortunately, he decided to listen to me and not blow up his marriage that night. When I hung up my pastor friend who was driving and listening to the entire conversation said "Wow! I have never talked to one of my guys like that!" I repeat that story not to say how great my counseling techniques were at the time, but to share an example of the difficult line pastors walk every day. When to take a stand, when to challenge a member's thinking or intended actions, when to risk losing the relationship. It is not an easy walk. My friend on the phone avoided any catastrophe to his marriage that night but his suspicions proved true over time. Years later they divorced. Pastors must respond in a way and a manner he or she believes is best for those in the church. Sometimes it works out, sometimes it does not but it is always a walk of faith. That is what is scripturally modeled and taught by other pastors in the faith. Not all those who attend a church learn that or live that way. But the church is still God's appointed place for the people of faith to gather and I love it in spite of its warts. Pastors compromise often, maybe too often. Consequently, in this ex-pastor's view the church drifts slowly from positions of faith once held. Violations of acceptable conduct by our elected officials go unchallenged and tolerated by exception time after time. Additionally, the higher the power of the elected official the less likely a pastor feels comfortable in challenging or criticizing because the larger the sphere of influence of the official then the greater the risk of impacting their local church. After a while, the pastor's logic that dominates is "what choice do I have?" In other words, the consequences of speaking out become too great, so one does not. The truth of the matter is we always have a choice to take a stand for truth. Let me quote my former youth pastor friend that I mentioned previously "It's always right to do right! It's never right to do wrong!" Makes things kind of simple. Sometimes it just takes a little courage to stand for what is commonly accepted as right, things like integrity, honesty, grace and kindness. How about expecting and requiring our elected officials to be reconcilers and not dividers, peacemakers not fighters? All of us in our faith communities should require at least that much. Maybe that would be a step toward "elect electing the elect".

We elect the leaders of our country. We expect our leaders to lead but often we do not demand it. The problem is most confuse leadership with management or charisma or some other personal quality. Leadership guides, shows the way, and inspires people to follow. We all admire as we should our fallen heroes who have made the ultimate sacrifice for their heroic leadership. Many of their testimonies are evidence of men and women leading others through perilous times and circumstances. That is what we expect a leader to do, but unfortunately we do not always require the same of our elected officials. Many times, we hear political analysts state that elected officials act or do not act in a manner so as not to offend a base of support of their constituency. That is understandable and acceptable for most occasions except when faced with perilous circumstances. When the way is confusing, conflicted, and perilous leaders must stand up and lead. A faith community should expect and demand our leaders to lead with integrity, honesty, compassion and most of all with the greater good in mind. Those qualities are the essence of Jesus' behavior and teachings. Some think leading a group to circumvent a constitutional election procedure is appropriate behavior for a leader of our country, but it is clear such actions do not have the greater good of the country in mind but rather one's personal interests only. Such self-centered conduct is destructive to the democracy of our nation and in my mind disqualifies the person responsible from any leadership position. I believe the welfare of our nation and its democracy are more critical and serve a higher priority than any politician's reelection.

Sometimes it takes courage to speak the truth, but it is always necessary if one is in a leadership position. The faith communities know this, or at least they should. Numbers 32:33 says in part "… your sin will find you out." Isaiah 59:4,5 is more explicit in its warning by stating "No one calls for justice, nor does any plead for truth. They trust in empty words and speak lies; they conceive evil and bring forth inequity. They hatch vipers' eggs and weave the spider's web; he who eats of their eggs dies, and from that which is crushed a viper breaks out." Jesus was a little more eloquent in His compassion in John 8:31.32 in saying "If you abide in My word, you are My disciples indeed. And you shall know the truth, and the truth shall make you free." We as a people of faith must demand truth from our elected officials at all times even if it is not what we want to hear. How can our leaders lead effectively if they are not leading truthfully? I know politics is a world of spin and half-truths where truth varies with one's perspective. One professional politician recently coined the now famous phrase "alternate facts". Facts are not variable; they do not change and they do not have alternatives. They are or are not facts. But we as the people of faith, the ones referred to as the "elect", must be better than that, we must demand more than that kind of nonsense. There is nothing wrong with the "elect" electing the "elect". That is, electing people that will tell the truth regardless, even if it is something we do not want to hear. Our leaders should not be constrained to tell us only what we feel is appropriate. They are elected to a position of higher authority with different exposure and perspective of national and world events. None of us who are parents would allow our teenager to make decisions that affect the welfare of our entire family. They simply do not have the exposure and view that we parents have. It is similar with our elected officials. We elect them to give us the truth based on their view from the highest governing position of our nation. Do not tell us what we want to hear to assure reelection, tell us the truth of our nation's business. If the communities of faith do not require this of our elected officials, then who will?

CHAPTER 12
Faith and the Constitution

"Congress shall make no law respecting an establishment of religion, or prohibiting the free exercise thereof;"
(Amendment 1 to the Constitution of the United States of America)

THE 2013 MOVIE "CAPTAIN PHILLIPS" STARRING TOM HANKS was the portrayal of the hijacking of the U.S. containership Maersk Alabama in April 2009 by Somali pirates. In his presidential memoirs, President Obama refers to the conclusion of the incident as follows. "But I also realized that around the world, in places like Yemen and Afghanistan, Pakistan and Iraq, the lives of millions of young men like those three dead Somalis (some of them boys, really, since the oldest pirate was believed to be nineteen) had been warped and stunted by desperation, ignorance, dreams of religious glory, the violence of their surroundings, or the schemes of older men. They were dangerous, these young men, often deliberately and casually cruel. Still in the aggregate, at least, I wanted to somehow to save them – send them to school, give them a trade, drain them of the hate that had been filling their heads. And yet the world they were a part of, and the machinery I commanded, more often had me killing them instead."[15] President Obama in his candid remarks on the incident refers to the complexity of governance and leading a nation when politics, religion, and the influences of those in control are mixed, particularly in an international context. However, this confluence of religion and politics or faith and governance is not only a complex international problem but a national one as well. The historical track record in our nation with regard to religion and politics has its share of tragedy. In President Lincoln's second inaugural address he describes the anguish between war and faith on both sides of the Civil War that was finally winding down but not yet concluded. Lincoln writes "Both parties deprecated war; but one of them would make war rather than let the nation survive; and the other would accept war rather than let it perish. And the war came."[16] Lincoln continues "Both read the same Bible and pray to the same God; and each invokes His against the other. It may seem strange that any men should dare to ask a just God's assistance in wringing their bread from the sweat of other men's faces; but let us judge not lest we be judged. The prayers of both could not be answered; that of neither has been answered fully. The Almighty has His own purposes."[17] Lincoln concludes "Yet, if God wills that it continue, until all the wealth piled by the bond-man's two hundred and fifty years of unrequited toil shall be sunk, and until every drop of blood drawn with the lash, shall be paid by another drawn with the sword, as was said three thousand years ago, so still it must be said "the judgements of the Lord, are true and righteous altogether.""[18] Both presidents remarking on the complexity of the outcomes on a nation when faith is mixed with the motives of some political actions. But how can this be when, I think it is safe to say,

---

[15] A Promised Land; by Barrack Obama; p.353; Crown of random House, 2020
[16] Every Drop of Blood; by Edward Achorn; p.297; Atlantic Monthly Press, 2020
[17] Ibid, p. 298
[18] Ibid, p. 298

faith and religion are clearly baked into the DNA of our nation and its governance. Jon Meacham writes "Dreams of God and gold (not necessarily in that order) made America possible. The First Charter of Virginia – the 1606 document that authorized the founding of Jamestown – is 3,805 words long. Ninety-eight of them are about carrying their religious faith to "such People, as yet live in Darkness and miserable Ignorance of the true Knowledge and Worship of God."[19] Of note in this charter is that faith was an important enough concern to be incorporated in this founding document and in my opinion in the right proportional amount of emphasis. That is the other 3,707 words or 97% of the document was dedicated to the governance of the colony. Likewise, the founding fathers of our nation made note of the value of freedom of religion in the first words of the First Amendment to the constitution as shown above. The first amendment continues to mention the other equally important freedoms of speech, press, assembly, and the petitioning of the Government. This with the other twenty-six amendments express the various liberties embedded in our constitution and available to us as part of our great nation. As was the case in the Jamestown charter, we also find in our constitution that freedom of religion is noted as one of the foremost liberties in the list of many offered, but not of any more equal value than the rest. This was by design based on the experience of our founding fathers coming from a nation with a state-sponsored faith. It was the intent for this new nation to be still under God but with a newly found freedom to worship however the people of this nation chose to do so.

There seems to be a different perspective by some in our nation today concerning faith and its religious practices and its relevance to the constitution. Du Mez writes "For conservative white evangelicals, the "good news" of the Christian gospel has been inextricably linked to a staunch commitment to patriarchal

---

[19] The Soul of America; by John Meacham; p.23; Merewether LLC, 2018

authority, gender difference and Christian nationalism, and all these are intertwined with white racial identity,"[20] Whitehead and Perry define Christian nationalism as "an ideology that idealizes and advocates a fusion of American civic life with a particular type of Christian identity and culture."[21] Whitehead and Perry assert that "Christian nationalism represents more than religion. It includes assumptions of nativism, white supremacy, patriarchy, and heteronormativity, along with divine sanction for authoritarian control and militarism. It is as ethnic and political as it is religious. Understood in this light, Christian nationalism contends America has been and should always be distinctively "Christian" from top to bottom – in its self-identity, interpretations of its own history, sacred symbols, cherished values, and public policies – and it aims to keep it that way."[22] Let me comment on this perspective of Christian nationalism in my own experience first, then how the issue relates to our topic of faith and the constitution as I understand it.

Whitehead and Perry's description of Christian nationalism is the result of two distinguished sociologists' effort that includes extensive research that is way beyond my scope of experience and even full understanding. That being said, I have been a part of the evangelical community of faith for many years. As I have explained previously, my specific faith journey has taken me to different aspects of that community; some may characterize those aspects as extreme opposite ends, from non-Pentecostal to Pentecostal denominations, within the evangelical community. I can affirm that in my faith experience in the 80's I heard some aspects of Christian nationalism advocated in that particular community. But since that early experience, the faith communities in which I have

---

[20] Jesus and John Wayne by Kristen Du Mez, p.6,7
[21] Taking America back for God; by Andrew Whitehead and Samuel Perry; P.ix-x, Oxford University Press; 2020.
[22] Ibid; P10.

participated, to include the pastoring of my own church, such views were not discussed or even mentioned that I can recall. That said, I know years ago and would suspect still today many evangelicals think of our nation as being a Christian nation or at least it should be considered a Christian nation. To be honest, I probably thought the same for many years, but like many aspects of my faith, it is a position that has changed for me over the years. I now believe that God's favor and blessings are implicit in all communities of faith, and I like to believe that was the position of our founding fathers when they scrolled the first amendment of the constitution using the words "make no law.... prohibiting the free exercise thereof (referring to the exercise of religion)." That is to say, all faiths have equal value and will have equal opportunity of expression in our great nation. However, a toxic blend of faith and politics has blurred these constitutional values in the view of many in our nation. I am not qualified to judge whether or not that blurring is a result of Christian nationalism. Regardless of its label, I believe this blurring of constitutional values has resulted in some alarming events throughout our nation over the last few years.

At this writing there has been a recent spike in anti-Semitic attacks throughout our country. The following excerpt from the New York Times alludes to a continuing problem in our nation that started as a political motivation in the past administration but has recently reached new fervor because of world events.

Incidents are "literally happening from coast to coast, and spreading like wildfire," said Jonathan Greenblatt, the A.D.L.'s chief executive. "The sheer audacity of these attacks feels very different." Until the latest surge, anti-Semitic violence in recent years was largely considered a right-wing phenomenon, driven by a white supremacist movement emboldened by rhetoric from former President Donald J. Trump, who often trafficked in stereotypes. Many of the most recent incidents, by contrast, have come from perpetrators expressing support for the Palestinian cause and criticism of Israel's right-wing government. "This is why Jews feel so terrified in this moment," Mr. Greenblatt said, observing that there are currents of anti-Semitism flowing from both the left and the right. "For four years it seemed to be stimulated from the political right, with devastating consequences" he noted.[23]

This blend of faith and political will has been nurtured in our nation over the last few years culminating on Jan.6, 2021 when a political rally turned into an assault on Capitol Hill. Prosecutions since that event have resulted in more than 600 of the charges being filed as potential felonies, and slightly more than half of the people being charged face at least one felony. Charges filed to date are in the following categories: assaulting or obstructing an officer (211); obstruction of an official proceeding (195); trespassing and possessing a weapon (112); theft or destruction of property (40); conspiracy (31); Other including interstate threats, possession of unregistered firearm or destructive device, and D.C weapons and theft charges (13).[24] What is most vexing to me is that while watching countless video of the events that day captured by the national media, occasional references to faith by some in the crowd could be heard. Phrases like "God's will" or "God sent us" would occasionally rise above all the shouting and screaming. At one point a glimpse of a cross being carried in the crowd could be seen near the Capitol. This is not to say that this was anywhere near a majority voice of the insurgents, but it was clear that the actions of some that day were motivated at least in part by their faith. When I see symbols of our faith community and hear references to God's

---

[23] "US Faces Outbreak of Ant-Semitic Threats and Violence" by Ruth Graham & Liam Stack; New York Times; May 26, 2021

[24] "A Sprawling Investigation into the Attack on the Capitol Gathers a Diverse Group of Suspects from Across the Nation" by Delvin Barrett, Abigail Hauslohner, Spencer S. Hsu and Ashlyn Still; Washington Post; May 16, 2021.

will as part of an insurrection against our government with the result being people injured and killed, I see a great erosion of the principles of our faith and how they relate to our constitution. Let me explain.

I view the constitution as a book of instructions running the operating system of our great nation called a democracy. The constitution guides the formulation of actions, procedures, and policies necessary to keep our democracy functioning as designed. Like any complex organization, system or organism there are certain processes or support functions more critical than others. For instance, arthritis in my hands and back have altered my golf game in its effectiveness but I still play. However, if I lost a limb or an eye my playing days would effectively be over. Likewise, if certain key functions are lost to our democracy, it becomes non-functional and no longer has the ability to govern as effectively as it did and in some extreme cases not at all. Our democratic election process is one such process that is critical to the functioning of our democracy and is defined by our constitution. Once this critical process is interrupted our country is no longer functioning according to our designed process by the constitution as a democracy, so the question then is what has our country become? The simple answer is that at the instant when the constitutional election process is broken, we have changed from a democracy to an autocracy. We have instantly changed from a balanced government consisting of an executive, legislative and judicial branch headed by an elected executive to a government with one person in charge and a legislative branch which lacks autonomy. In that moment all the blood that has been shed over the years in the spirit of preserving our democratic way of life has been in vain. Here is the point that I want to make as a former pastor in a faith community and a former federal government civil servant. If our faith has directly or indirectly made us complicit in a crisis like this that causes the destruction of our democracy protected by the same constitution that protects our freedom of religion, then we have truly lost our way as a nation and a people of faith.

We must hold on to the precious truths that keep our nation intact. Our country is still in its infancy when compared to many countries around the globe. We are still an experiment in the eyes of the world, waiting to see how long we can survive. I believe in God, and I believe His favor is on our nation and many others. But my life faith experience tells me that our faith does not exclude us from consequences made by our poor judgement. Just as the constitution demands that "Congress shall make no law respecting an establishment of religion or prohibiting the free exercise thereof" conversely our faith demands we evangelicals take no action stopping the effective working of our constitution that preserves our democracy and our nation. The constitution casts an umbrella of protection over our right to practice our religion and prohibits any actions preventing that right. Conversely our faith should demand that any expression of our faith or religious belief should not jeopardize our constitution no matter how remotely or indirectly.

I cannot leave this discussion of our constitution and faith without talking about the second amendment. Du Mez notes "Writers on evangelical masculinity have long celebrated the role guns play in forging Christian manhood. From toy guns in childhood to real firearms gifted in initiation ceremonies, guns are seen to cultivate authentic, God-given masculinity. A 2017 survey revealed that 41 percent of white evangelicals' own guns, a number higher than members of any other faith group and significantly higher than the 30 percent of Americans overall who own firearms."[25]

Personally, guns have never interested me. My only experience

---

[25] Jesus and John Wayne by Kristen Du Mez, p.296

with them is the requisite training on the rifle range as part of my ROTC program in college. I have never owned a gun and probably never will. Additionally, my faith experience cannot confirm or deny Du Mez's research because the faith communities that I have been involved with never had any association with guns. That is reasonable given that most of my experience has been in the suburban community of the Washington D.C. area. However, I have a close friend who is a former college classmate who has a completely different experience. He is a hunter, owns a wide range and variety of guns while being a very devout evangelical man of faith. He still attends services every Sunday at the church where he and his wife were married almost 50 years ago. On a recent visit I asked him why some needed automatic weapons to hunt deer, that being the popular prey of choice in his area of our country. His response was that simply some hunters are zealots. I understand that because I am zealous when it comes to my hobby of golf. The only difference is that as far as I know there has never been a mass murder of folks using a golf club. I know I am being extremely cynical, but I think the topic requires some cynicism at this point in our nation's history with guns. I will not take the time to repeat the staggering numbers of annual deaths in our nation caused by automatic weapons. It is a unique issue that has plagued our nation for many years that touches the boundaries of constitutional liberty, faith and politics. Let us quickly look at all these perspectives.

I am fully aware of the constitutional argument that is presented justifying automatic weapons in our country as it clearly states that "the right of the people to keep and bear Arms, shall not be infringed." I get it. What I do not get is ignoring the words that start the second amendment and precede those just quoted. Those initial words are: "A well-regulated Militia, being necessary to the security of a free State". By introducing the amendment in this manner our founding fathers were establishing the conditions that required the people of this nation to bear arms. That is, it was a necessary right to keep weapons in one's home because the only means of a national defense was the volunteer militia. There was no Department of Defense to protect our country from invasion. Moreover, there was no state, county, or local police force as well to protect the people from civil threats. Guns were required to be in the home because the residents were on call at any time to defend themselves and their country from any known and unknown threat. It makes perfect sense. However, as insightful as these men were, I am sure they never imagined stocking homes with more than the equivalent firepower of the First Continental Army. In fact, some inference to this type of concern can be drawn from the third amendment that states "No soldier shall, in time of peace be quartered in any house, without the consent of the Owner, nor in time of war, but in a manner to be prescribed by law." This amendment reflects a concern over the threat of a military capability taking up residence in private homes without the appropriate prescription of law permitting it. I would suggest we have those military equivalent capabilities and more in many households in our nation today without the adequate protection to the people of this nation. The evidence is in the news on a daily basis.

I am not against guns. What I am against is how the understanding of this constitutional right has been extorted, misrepresented, and blurred all for the sake of political power. The influence of the gun lobby on Capitol Hill is no secret. Consequently, political campaigns promote fear of the legislation designed to further protect society from violent gun assaults. They do so by misrepresenting the intent of such legislation as being designed to take away a constitutional right. Curtailing our liberties for the protection of society is an act of choosing the greater good and is exercised frequently in our American experience. Many of us like to drive fast, but we willingly submit to speed limits for the greater good. Many of us enjoy an occasional beer or dinner cocktail and we willingly submit to limits in our alcoholic consumption in public and while driving for the greater good. Many of us love to go to movies or ballgame and get emotionally involved shouting or cheering, but we willingly submit to a restraint in language for the greater good. I cannot understand why even the greatest gun advocate would not willingly submit to curtailing some gun liberties for the greater good. It is not a violation of a constitutional right to do so, it is quite the opposite. It is an act of protecting the constitution that guarantees all of our liberties. Let me quote from the start of our constitution: "We the People of the United States, in Order to form a more perfect Union, establish Justice, insure domestic Tranquility, provide for the common defence, promote the general Welfare, and secure the Blessings of Liberty to ourselves and our Posterity, do ordain and establish this Constitution for the United States of America," Let me ask how our domestic tranquility can be insured, our common defense be provided, and the general welfare be promoted for our nation with the current onslaught of gun violence in our country? These are the sacrifices of our constitutional rights for the political power of some elected officials.

Again, my argument is not with elected political officials. They simply represent the people that elect them. My argument is with the people of faith who submit to this false constitutional argument as the reason to oppose any gun legislation. The issue really has nothing to do with the constitution for people of faith, it is an issue of the sanctity of life. My issue is this. If one's faith defines the beginning of life as a fetus, then I see no difference between the taking of a life through an abortion and taking a life with an assault weapon. If I am moved enough to demonstrate against abortion by carrying signs of an aborted fetus then my faith should compel me to demonstrate to the same degree when kindergarten children are innocently gunned down, or a crowd is fired upon during a concert or an entire congregation is killed during a prayer meeting. I see no difference, yet I see no equivalent outrage in the people of faith. I call that hypocrisy. The only time Jesus was moved to violence himself was in the face of the hypocrisy of the people of faith in the temple (John 2:13-16).

Anyone who has followed professional football even in a casual way has probably caught a glimpse of a ritual that frequently occurs after a game when players from both teams gather in a circle on bended knee, holding hands, heads bowed in prayer. I have never been in one of those circles but can guess the general atmosphere is one of thankfulness for continued physical health after having just competed in an honest competition and a spirit of unity in faith for those in the circle. I marvel at the sight every time because just minutes before those same athletes had been using all their energy pushing each other all over the field with all the competitive juices they could summon for several hours. Each player is invested in their team's approach, strategy and a belief that they have it right and their opponent has it a little bit wrong, giving them a competitive edge and belief they are the better team that day. If not, they know they will not be in that league very long. But when the game is over, they all become united in their common faith. Why does it seem we cannot come together as a faith community when it comes to politics? Our faith communities have parsed scriptures to the extent that we have divided the soul of our nation and retreated to our respective political teams. Our constitution gives us the luxury and freedom to do just that. But in this case the outcome at stake is more than a game – it is our democracy. Our nation and our religious freedom cannot continue to exist unless we abide by and make every effort to preserve and protect our constitution. That is the oath every president takes when he assumes the office elected by the people of this nation. We cannot let the outcomes of our faith

PART 4
FAITH FOR THE TIMES

"And from the days of John the Baptist until now the kingdom of heaven suffers violence, and the violent take it by force. For all the prophets and the law prophesied until John. And if you are willing to receive it, he is Elijah who is to come. He who has ears to hear, let him hear!" Mathew 11:12-14

The natural and the supernatural co-exist, with each mostly unnoticed until by some set of unpredictable circumstances they intersect. The natural blends into our everyday routine experience and by so doing becomes invisible. At one time I lived on the bank of a reservoir with a breath-taking view as the water wrapped around the corner of my deck and was visible in both direction for miles. The first time I walked into the house I was awe-struck with the beauty visible from every level of the house. After living there for a period of time I stopped even noticing the view. I do not really remember exactly when I stopped "seeing" the water but at some point, it disappeared. Of course, it was still physically there but it had vanished from my conscious awareness and at that point I hardly noticed it. That is our natural existence. On the other hand, the supernatural is never seen, only felt when it intersects with the natural. These intersections are spontaneous but do not occur without some preparation of the mind, heart and soul. They are instantaneous in experience but lasting in effect and sometimes life altering. They are those events when hearts, behaviors, attitudes or habits that have been a part of us for longer than we can remember suddenly change. They are events that may be life altering and in ways that we do not understand or welcome in our lives. The drunken sobers. The addicted family member overdoses. The marriage is reconciled. A family member is lost in a random act of gun violence. The estranged are united. A cancer is healed. A hidden life is revealed. A life is lost. Inexplicable events, unpredictable and completely out of one's control to make it begin or end. I have tried to understand these events through the lens of my faith. All of those experiences, good or bad. I find that scriptures' many metaphors help me understand in some small way more about this phenomenon. "But those who wait on the Lord, shall renew their strength, they shall mount up with wings like eagles, they shall run and not be weary, they shall walk and not faint" (Isaiah 40:31). Yea, though I walk through the valley of the shadow of death, I will fear no evil; for You are with me;" (Psalm 23:4). Two of my favorites, but my best is 1 Kings 19:11-13. "Then He said, "Go out, and stand on the mountain before the Lord." And behold, the Lord passed by, and a great and strong wind tore into the mountains and broke the rocks in pieces before the Lord, but the Lord was not in the wind; and after the wind an earthquake, but the Lord was not in the earthquake; and after the earthquake a fire; and after the fire a still small voice. So it was, when Elijah heard it, that he wrapped his face in his mantle and went out and stood in the entrance of the cave. And suddenly a voice came to him, and said, "What are you doing here, Elijah?""

The literal translation in this reference is "a delicate whispering voice". In those moments that are larger than life, when things are changing all around, these are the events that I call the intersection of the natural with the supernatural. In those moments I believe our faith is activated through the experience, often in a delicate whispering voice. A voice that begins requiring some reflection and self-examination. A voice that then speaks comfort to our soul, wisdom for the moment and direction for the time.

I believe our evangelical communities of faith are in the midst of a perilous time. Faith is in decline; contentions are on the rise and divisions in the communities of faith have not been greater. I believe we need to hear that delicate whispering voice to bring about change to the people of faith. What is needed is a faith experience that fosters the intersection of the natural with the supernatural to hear that voice. A voice that will first require some self-examination. A voice that will stir the souls of the faith community, asking "what are we doing here?" We need to hear that voice to heal and for a new direction of unity in faith. This intersection is not to be evidenced through catastrophe or disaster, but through effectual prayer, worship, and praise when the people of faith assemble. An assembly that recognizes the need to move away from an emphasis on learning about faith and allows a time and opportunity to experience faith. This would require a shift in form and substance in the evangelical communities of faith. First, we must change our focus in the faith communities from the platform to the pew. Next, we must realize a sense of urgency to act. Finally, we must be open to new methods and outcomes. In this final part I will discuss some suggestions on how to move in those directions. New directions are not easy but sometimes necessary. Jesus described the introduction of His own ministry to the community of faith at that time as a "violent" undertaking referring to His literal suffering and shedding of His blood prophetically. As a point of emphasis, He invoked the messages of all the prophets from Elijah to John the Baptist to substantiate the change He was representing. But most of all He said it would take a community of faith that had the spiritual ears to "hear" the call for change. I believe we are in a similar season of change. All that is required in this instance is the ability to "hear" the summons to change. My hope is that there are ears to "hear" as I do.

CHAPTER 13
Pew verses Platform

I CAN REMEMBER THE EXCITEMENT LEADING UP TO THAT FIRST Sunday service pastoring the church I started in the fall of 1999. I had earnestly prepared that first sermon for weeks, convinced it would be so powerful and transformative that it would compel all those who heard it to return week after week bringing family and friends. In my mind that is all it would take to launch a successful ministry, along with some initial vigorous campaigning of family, friends and contacts that had been nurtured over the years of ministering locally at several churches. The effort for that first service paid dividends with approximately one-hundred folks turning out to the recreation center rented for the event. Every available folding chair in the place was used that morning and I was pumped! Little did I know what a tough journey would lie ahead during the next seven years. It began to occur to me that it was not going to be as easy as I thought it would be the very next week when twenty-seven souls returned for the second service. Little did I know that would be the pattern over the life of this church start-up, as it is for many like it. There would be periodic services with large attendance as a result of some all-out effort that included food, special attractions and a lot of advertising. Only for attendance to dramatically fall off quickly after the event. I once calculated the seven-year attendance average of my church to be slightly under thirty per week. I was doing church the way I had experienced it for many years. That is, the service was being conducted with the platform being the focus, even though in my case there was not a literal platform. What I mean is that the service presentation was predominately lead and controlled by the pastor up front. There was some delegation of responsibilities in music, nursery duty and social services such as refreshments, greeting and most of all getting contact information from any visitors. I have been in many evangelical churches over the years, and all followed this general conduct of service with slight variations. The larger the church, the more effective the platform presentation. More professional musicians, experienced vocalists and better sound systems result in a better platform presentation. Along with those benefits, larger churches offer additional services for nursery and childcare, and in some cases have special features for teens that all combine for a wonderful experience for the entire family resulting in attracting larger audiences. Larger audiences offer a larger pool of resources and volunteers all contributing to a more effective ministry. A smaller church, in particular one just starting, has a difficult time competing with larger churches, particularly if you are located in the suburbs of a major city as was mine. Most independent churches start from humble beginnings. Those that succeed usually take the lifetime effort of more than one senior pastor. Lakewood Church, located in Houston, Texas is one of the largest congregations in the nation, averaging about 52,000 attendees per week. Pastor Joel Osteen took over as senior pastor after the death of his father, who founded the church many years earlier in the back of a feed store. Both pastors labored for years to bring the church to the place it is today. I have never been to Lakewood Church but have been to several with large congregations and have had many wonderful spiritual experiences in them. But I believe the vast number of churches in our nation are small in comparison. Google will tell you that in 2012 the average congregation had only seventy regular participants, adults and children, and an annual budget of $85,000. The point being that with church services being platform centric, most churches in our nation (like mine was) do not have the resources to have an elaborate presentation and are extremely limited in the services provided. Most churches are limited to the innovation of the local pastor to try and make each service interesting, entertaining, and at the same time effectively utilizing any volunteer labor available. If that is not enough of a challenge, communicating scriptural principles to an audience is a complex task that even the Apostle Paul struggled with at times. In Acts 20:9 we see Paul teaching for such a prolonged time that a young man falls asleep and falls "from the third story was taken up dead." Fortunately, that never happened to me, and in Paul's case he was able to revive the young lad. This account illustrates the principle widely known that most people's attention span during a lecture is ten to twenty minutes. When I was teaching high school math, we were instructed to vary our instructional methods and activities every twenty minutes. That was quite a challenge when teaching multiple classes with multiple subjects each day but necessary to try and keep the student's attention for a ninety-minute class. More often than not I would see students' heads crashing asleep to their desks in spite of my best efforts. The church audience is not any different.

The church experience has become platform-centric, at the expense of holding the interest of the listening audience sitting in the pews, or in the case of my church sitting in folding chairs. Pastors, constrained in time, and with multiple services, tightly control the agenda to be sure to cover all the requisite aspects of church business. Encouraging participation in the various church activities, advocating support of church affiliates as part of the denominational responsibilities and taking financial offerings are all necessary for the continued life flow of the church. In addition, acknowledging births, deaths, marriages, graduations, Mother's Day, Father's Day and Veteran's Day are all vital in the promotion of a community which is a critical outcome of a church experience. All that is wonderful, and I enjoyed doing all those activities as a pastor, but each moment spent in such acknowledgements diminishes the amount of time available to building up and ministering to the souls sitting in the pews. The result is that the likelihood of nurturing a significant spiritual event, one that touches hearts, heals souls and builds faith becomes less and less. Such events, what I call the intersection of the natural with the supernatural, do not happen quickly. They are encounters that must be nurtured and not rushed. They are not subject to our timetables and our demands. They cannot be managed, only waited for in hopeful anticipation. The model for this type of service is described in Acts 2:1,2 at what I believe is the first assembly of the first New Testament church. "Now when the day of Pentecost had fully come, they were all in one accord in one place. And suddenly there came a sound from heaven, as a rush of a mighty wind, and it filled the whole house where they were sitting." One accord in one place means they were gathered in unity of mind and spirit. We do not know exactly what the activities were when these faithful gathered. I suspect some were praying. Maybe there was some singing and worship. Probably many were sitting silently contemplating the moment. I suspect there was a common expectation as they no doubt had gathered at that exact time, based on promises and indications made during the earthly ministry of Jesus. Now they were alone in their faith, patiently waiting, anticipating what was to follow, not knowing for sure when or what that would be, but trusting that it was what was required to move on in their faith. Scripture gives us no indication that any one individual was in charge; that there was no special agenda or designated topic of discussion or teaching. There was no one preaching or teaching from a platform every moment they were there; the focus was collectively on the individuals in the pews.

I have been in church services that are similar to the one described above. Not that they were as meaningful or as significant as Pentecost was to the universal church (described in Acts 2) but they were very meaningful experiences to me. I have elaborated on some of those experiences in previous chapters. My most meaningful church experiences have been those in which the focus of the service moved from the platform to the pew. By that I mean from the beginning of the service no one was in control. There was someone leading the service but not controlling it. The service would transition in leadership seamlessly between an individual leading worship and an individual that would lead in the exhortation of the gathered community to pray individually or collectively or sit silently as the moment dictated. There was a freedom to experience the presence of God in any way that was comfortable for the individual. My first experience of this type of service occurred very naturally in an impromptu way in a church for which that was not the normal custom. It was a special intimate moment during which the guest speaker scheduled for that day declined to speak in deference to the moment. It was like Acts 2 and it was such an experience that it created a spiritual hunger in that local faith community to experience it again and again. As this type of service began to trend to a new norm in this church, not all agreed with the change. In order for an environment like this to exist spiritually there must be general agreement as in Acts 2 "they were all in one accord". Resistance grew and quickly the services returned back to the normal platform-centered type of service. That experience illustrated to me a spiritual principal that I have never forgotten that applies to church services and individuals alike.

CHAPTER 14

Such a Time as This

"YET WHO KNOWS WHETHER YOU HAVE COME TO THE KINGDOM for such a time as this?" (Esther 4:14) The referenced question is from the wonderful biblical account that occurred during a time when there were Jewish exiles throughout the Persian Empire. The question is at the end of an appeal by a gentleman named Mordecai to his adopted daughter Esther who had been selected as queen because of her great beauty. Mordecai's request was for Esther to go to the king and request him to intervene in a plot to kill all the Jews in Persia. The only catch was that Esther had not been summoned by the king and the rule was that anyone entering the king's presence without a summons would risk being sent to die unless the king opted not to do so, i.e., catch him in a good mood. You can imagine Esther's concern and reluctance. As the story goes, she eventually did what she was asked to do, was spared by the king and was successful in stopping the plot to kill the Jews. We can look at an example like this after the fact and say what is the big deal? Of course, the king was not going to kill his beautiful queen, right? But I am sure from Esther's point of view it took great courage to act, at great personal risk. The circumstances dictated that somebody needed to take some action. I am no Queen Esther and I do not believe our nation is on the "eve of destruction" as was sung by Barry McGuire back in 1965. But I do sense an increased aggression and hostility in our nation as we turn on each other, American against American, and in many cases people of faith. Conflict among faith communities is nothing new, but I believe at this point in time that the inherent risk to our nation is great because of these conflicts. Specifically, the "polarization of faith" discussed previously is driving a larger and larger wedge between faith communities. The result is the emboldening of political officials all across our nation proposing legislation that if enacted will routinely overturn elections and nullify our constitutional right of elections by the people. Additionally, we have U.S. Senators openly stating their main objective while in Congress is to oppose any legislation proposed by the opposing political party and to obstruct the legislative process. These are crises of governance that I believe are largely enabled by what I call an *identity crisis* of the evangelical people of faith. Let me explain.

We evangelicals identify ourselves by a set of common core beliefs that mostly have their basis in scripture. Choose any evangelical community website regardless of the denomination and somewhere on that site will be a set of core beliefs. Looking further into the various faith communities these core beliefs are translated into doctrines that guide the behaviors of the particulars of that faith community. For example, as a child in parochial school I was taught that the Catholic Church was the one true church. Later on in life, as part of an independent Baptist community I was taught that Catholics were not really Christians (at least not like us Baptists) and that Pentecostals were deceived in what they believed. Maybe Pentecostals were Christian but there was something not right with them. And yet later when I became a Pentecostal, I learned that some Catholics and Baptists were Pentecostal as well, just like us, but not all of them. This experience alone would lead anyone to conclude that there is an *identity conflict* within the evangelical community. The truth of the matter is that this identity conflict has existed for many years and probably always will. This conflict is a result of different interpretations of scriptural meaning, context or application. I had the experience of reading the same scriptures as a Baptist and a Pentecostal and understanding them differently according to the community to which I belonged at the time. These liberties should be allowed according to each person's measure of faith. However, an *identity conflict* is different from an *identity crisis*. An *identity crisis* occurs when an erosion of core values has such an effect on the outcomes of our faith that we are without distinction from people without faith. The distinguishing values of our faith communities are many and are often repeated throughout the apostle Paul's epistles to the churches of Corinth, Colosse, Phillipi and Ephesus as well as in his other New Testament writings. But the simplest and most profound distinction for me as fitting for our times is found in Colossians 4:5,6. "Walk in wisdom toward those who are outside, redeeming the time. Let your speech always be with grace, seasoned with salt, that you may know how you ought to answer each one." What Paul is saying is that the biggest impact we of faith can have on those who have no faith is with our words. Not just any words, but kind words absent of rancor, bitterness, and anger. It is only when those sorts of words occupy our minds and hearts that God gives us the grace and wisdom to know how to respond, how to answer the many questions that confront us in our nation today. Paul makes his case that if we make intelligent decisions regarding how we communicate to those who have no faith the result will be "redeeming the time". The literal translation means to "buy back" some time. What Paul is intimating is, that if we speak that way, people will listen and give us further opportunity to speak or speak again at another time. I believe our nation is desperate for this kind of civil discourse. We have lived through a season when the discourse from the highest levels of our nation has been absent of grace, kindness, understanding and most of all wisdom, precisely those qualities that invite communication. No wonder nobody is listening to each other.

It occurs to me that what is needed now is not another theological debate but simply a statement made through action. I have come to this point of view having been well-schooled in the evangelical doctrine of faith through years of study and teaching, a graduate degree, and a lifetime of faithful weekly, even several times a week, church attendance. The results of these experiences have produced arguments and counterarguments within my soul that have resulted in the point of view that has settled in my heart and mind at this time. But I have grown tired of the debate. Moreover, I am convinced that the people of our nation have grown tired of the debate as well. The evidence of this is the general state of the evangelical church today. That is, more have left the church then remain in it. Most evangelicals go occasionally and casually without purpose or passion. Most of the work is done by a few. I have been taught to believe that this is the natural order of things. The result of the proverbial war of good versus evil. But I have come to believe that this is the result of an empty message causing a faith community to lose its effectiveness, moving from spirit led to a preference of being authoritarian ruled. I believe that "such a time as this" would find a faith community receptive to a new method, a new emphasis, a plan of action that would introduce a new spirit into all the communities of faith throughout our nation.

When I was pastoring, a well-meaning member of my church introduced me to a homeless single mother of six. He came across this family hitch-hiking and not knowing how to help them he brought them to my door. What followed was a faith journey for my small church. At first members took turns housing portions of this family in different homes. Then the church housed the family in a local hotel while looking for a permanent solution. Finally, a government subsidized house, adequate to comfortably accommodate the whole family near school and work, was found. Church members moved the family into the home and continued to provide periodic transportation for them. The experience left the church exhausted of our savings and more educated about unconditional giving, especially when the family eventually stopped attending services at our church. I later learned that this lady had exploited the grace of other churches before ours. Most churches either dropped them off at a shelter or paid a couple of nights in a motel. I thought of doing the same many times during the long ordeal, but I just could not turn from this family. The situation was desperate, and somebody had to take some action to remedy the situation long term. I believe our small community of faith did just that for "such a time as this". Maybe someday I will know what impact we had on that family – maybe not – but that is ok. I believe that when times are desperate action is required. That is how I feel about our nation and its current state. I do not think the solution is political but spiritual. The solution will not come from politicians but from people of faith and their respective communities of faith for "such a time as this!"

CHAPTER 15
Different Methods for Different Outcomes

⁓

AS I APPROACH MY FIFTH YEAR OF RETIREMENT, I ENDEAVOR TO continue on my journey of faith which began in the first grade. Much has changed in form and function from those early years and what I believe today is vastly different from those early formative days. I believe this is the natural progression of faith. I believe faith is active and alive. If our faith is not growing and maturing, then it is static and stagnating. This is what I believe Paul is alluding to when he says, "the righteousness of God is revealed from faith to faith" (Romans 1:17). This progression has permitted me to experience different communities of faith. Each of these communities has similarities and differences. As mentioned before, differences are attributed to slightly different doctrinal positions that effect the customs and ordinances of that particular community. Similarities are usually in governance and organizational structure. All the main denominations are highly organized with hierarchical structures and governing bodies. These structures determine the limits and extent of acceptable boundaries of the conduct of the community. This includes an acceptable manner of worship, interpretation of scripture context and meaning, and defining the ordinances to be followed by the community. All are established by the hierarchy to permit consistency throughout the community of faith. Spontaneity and new revelation are tolerated as an acceptable norm only with the approval of the governing body. For example, one of the communities that I was a part of for many years was an international organization of over 69,000,000 members, approximately 400,000 churches in approximately 190 countries. Some of my most meaningful spiritual moments were experienced in two of these churches in different locations in our country. I have been in several other churches of this denomination over the years, and it is safe to say that those services in which I had those unique experiences were not routine services. There was a departure from the customary order and content of the service that was approved by the local church governance. There was no requirement of universal denominational approval for a fresh experience with God. But as I also mentioned, these services were outside the norm of the church worship and eventually the church returned to its customary form of service. The point is that these highly organized denominations offer many wonderful experiences to many people of faith but there are also constraints. For most church attendees these constraints are not an issue. For someone like myself, my faith experience was limited by the constraints of this denomination and others in which I had previously been a member. Let me explain.

When I started my church, it was not done on a whim. The desire to pastor had been welling up in my soul for years. However, that was impossible in every denomination in which I participated, because I had been married previously. It did not seem to matter that my first wife was deceased before I remarried. The discrediting fact was that I was divorced before I was widowed. That was perceived as a fatal blemish to licensing and ordination. That did not extinguish the desire, so I continued to study and prepare. When the desire to act became greater than waiting I started my church as an independent Pentecostal church. The only guidance I had was God tugging at my heart and fueling a desire to go in faith. A few years after starting, I was introduced to a Pentecostal denomination that made exceptions to divorce on a case-by-case basis. After passing several board interviews and fulfilling a couple of denominational training requirements I was licensed and ordained in the International Pentecostal Holiness Church (IPHC) an international church in ninety-five nations with 1,500,000 members and over 1,600 IPHC congregations in the United States. Being accepted into an international denomination that was founded in the 1890's was one of the highest honors in my life, certainly the highest as a minster in the evangelical community of faith.

Belonging to a larger denomination infrastructure offered many resources previously not available to an independent church. Training, camps, conferences, and retreats were now routinely available to any member of my church interested in such events. It also offered a covering of authority for me as a pastor in case of difficulties with members or any of the myriad of challenges a pastor confronts. However, these resources come with a financial cost. In this denomination, as is the case in most, all the pastor's giving goes to the denomination that previously went to my own church. Additionally, a portion of the church's income also went to support the denomination. In a small church like mine, finances were quickly constrained limiting the ability to pay part time staff and to reach out to the local community. Once financial pressures start, a labor that was never easy becomes more strained and difficult. Often the pastor resorts to pressuring the congregation to meet financial obligations which predictably releases a spirit of despair in a small community of faith. What was once a shared labor of love suddenly is perceived as an obligation. Then it is only a matter of time before the inevitable fate of many church start-ups occurs. The church closes its doors.

The above account could be construed as the disappointed experience of an ex-pastor. But I have seen and heard this story many times. I know many pastors who have been disillusioned and burnt out from similar experiences. To be honest, I went through a season of exhaustion and bitterness after my church closing. But in the years since I have come full circle and believe that I have a good perspective on the merits of this experience. I believe the current church industry is an invaluable resource. Many churches offer an opportunity for multitudes of people to experience community and grow in their faith. They are excellent places for someone like me to be launched in a faith journey. A well-established church is functional enough to withstand the ebb and flow of people coming and going through its doors. I do not know current statistics, but when I was pastoring a church had to recruit an additional ten percent of people each year just to make up for normal attrition. Of course, these percentages vary among churches, but the point is that a certain number of new members must come into a church every year or the church will eventually become unviable and close. So, someone like me can walk into an established church and grow in their faith as much as he or she wants. If that faith journey leads that person to another church, so be it. These well-established churches are perfect beds of spiritual growth for people to experience and stay or move on. But why then are the overall numbers of church members in decline? I believe it is because the nature of faith is that it must grow, "faith to faith", as I mentioned in the beginning of this chapter. If one's faith is not growing it is dying. Our spiritual life parallels our physical life. If we do not exercise and treat our bodies correctly, they atrophy and are subject to all sorts of vulnerabilities. The older one gets, the harder we must work to preserve a normal healthy life. It is the same with our spirit and soul. They must be nurtured, maintained and exercised in order to continue functioning vibrantly. What I believe is needed now is a new dimension to be added to our faith communities. Not replacing but to come along side those churches that are thriving and where people are growing in their faith; places where faith can be enhanced by an experience of faith; places that nurture the intersection of the natural with the supernatural; places that will not replace the teaching of the history and doctrine of our faith but add to it with additional experiences of faith outside the customary routine of church; places of faith where one can attend in anticipation of having an experience with God. I believe the faith communities in our nation are starved for this type of actionable faith!

What I propose are faith communities in an informal association, a network only associated by its approach to the faith experience. An association of communities that informally communicates through social media a general listing of gatherings, when and where they occur. Communities where the range of worship experiences can run from silence to shouts of praise, all during the same experience as the moment demands. The approach would consist of informal gatherings in homes and other designated places where the focus would be on worship, prayer for one another and being open to experiencing the presence of God. By that I mean an environment that nurtures the presence of God by not being constrained with a required format or common methodology. They would be faith communities that are not controlled by denominational constraints but led by local appointed leaders that are like-minded and like-hearted in this endeavor, that are trusted to lead a community in a meaningful faith experience. I am describing a contemporary version of the Acts 2 experience where people were gathered with one accord in one place, with no infrastructure to support, no pre-planned campaign to raise money to support some noble cause, no predetermined sermon or series of teachings to clarify some scriptural concept. They would simply be a people of faith, gathering when felt called to do so, to experience an intersection of the natural with the supernatural. It would be a time when lives can be touched and changed because we need it so desperately for our families, our communities and our nation. A new method for a new outcome!

EPILOGUE

I LOVE MY ITALIAN HERITAGE AND HAVE MANY WONDERFUL memories of growing up in a traditional Italian family. Holidays and special occasions were filled with family and lots of food. Traditionally holidays ended with a card game for the men; pinochle was the game of choice. We knew the evening was over when the card game concluded, usually with a lot of shouting over who made a bonehead move accompanied with a lot of hugs, backslapping and laughs. But these traditions came with a strict, authoritarian up-bringing for me and my brother. Expectations were high concerning grades in school and performance in athletics. There were rules for everything including clothes, haircuts and especially our conduct. A strong work ethic was introduced early in life with chores around the house of weeding, lawn cutting and other odd jobs. Both my brother and I were introduced into the workforce as soon as we were eligible, working summers and sometimes during school breaks. Then I found myself as a young adult somewhat rigid, stoic, and very shy in my social interactions. Most of all, as mentioned before, I found myself with an ever-present anger deep within my soul that would emerge occasionally. It left me sullen, moody, and very often I retreated within my own head, isolated and distant from even my closest relationships. I am not that person today. I try hard to communicate with all my relationships and am openly affectionate to my loved ones. I cry often now – not in sadness but out of joy. I cry watching movies, when I hear Anthony Bocelli sing or when I hear a compassionate story of self-sacrifice. I was not always this way. I attribute the reshaping of my heart and emotions to my faith journey. I am extremely grateful to every minister and community of faith that I have known and been a part of over the years. I love and respect the evangelical church at large. It is that love for the church that still compels me to add to it and to encourage people in their faith, to evangelize. That is the reason for this writing, in the hope of planting the seed for a faith community that accommodates more experience with God and not one just limited to information about God. I have tried to present an argument for that need in the church today through my personal experiences and my observations of our nation today. It has been a pleasure for me to express my thoughts without constraint. I hope they have been helpful in some way.

I will leave you with this one final experience and thought. I taught public high school math for five-plus years, starting as a long-term substitute teaching a general math/pre-algebra course. There was a young lady in that class who had a hard time grasping the general concepts of the class. Math did not come easily to her, but she persevered each year. I had the good fortune of teaching her again her senior year. In her final math exam in high school, she ended up scoring an A which pulled her final grade up to an A for the year. On one of the last days of school she came by my classroom and handed me a handwritten note. In her note she pointed out I was the only math teacher she had had for all her courses, a fact that I had not known until that moment. She thanked me and stated she would always regard me as her math teacher. Her note made all my difficulties as a math teacher worthwhile, for that is the heart of every educator. That is, to be remembered as a teacher that has had an impact on a student. Pastors feel the same way. They simply want to impact lives with what they have learned. I hope this writing will impact some life some time. That is my heart's desire.

BIBLIOGRAPHY

Achorn, Edward, "Every Drop of Blood", Atlantic Monthly Press (March 2020)

Carney, Timothy P., "Alienated America", Harper Collins (2019)

Du Mez, Kristen Kobes, "Jesus and John Wayne – How White Evangelicals Corrupted a Faith and Fractured a Nation", Liveright Publishing Corporation (2020)

Klein, Ezra, "Why We're Polarized", Avid Reader Press (2020)

Meacham, John, "The Soul of America – the Battle for our Better Angels", Random House (2018)

Meacham, John, "The Hope of Glory – Reflections on the Last Words of Jesus from the Cross", Convergent Books (2020)

Obama, Barrack, "A Promised Land", Random House (2020)

Whitehead, Andrew L. and Perry, Samuel L., "Taking America Back for God", Oxford University Press (2020)

INDEX

READER'S GUIDE

This guide may serve as a tool to promote group discussion about this book. It includes a short description of the content of each chapter and some sample questions that may help facilitate discussion.

Chapter 1 – Faith Revealed Generation to Generation

This chapter illustrates the author's experience as to how faith was and is being passed from generation to generation. Group discussion should focus on how faith was, is and will be passed in the group's generational experiences.

- What faith experience has been passed down through the generations in your family?
- How are you actively trying to pass on a faith tradition in your family?
- Do you agree or disagree with the author's approach to a discussion about life after death? What is your approach to discuss life after death?

Chapter 2 – Faith Revealed through Sacrifice

This chapter illustrates that faith is a critical part of the nature and extent of sacrifice that an individual is willing to make in his life and how faith is active in several types of sacrifice. The first type of sacrifice described is through some occupation or service (military, medical, social). The next type discussed is event based when someone literally risks their life for the benefit of someone else. The last type discussed is a lifestyle of routinely investing in the lives of family and friends around you either through actions or charitable giving.

- What are some of your experiences of faith through sacrifice?
- How does faith influence the nature and extent of sacrifice willing to be made? Do you agree or disagree with the author's position that we each have a limited reserve of faith available for traumatic circumstances? Please explain.
- Would you consider incorporating the topic of sacrifices made during one's life to a family member who is terminally ill? Why or why not? Extended family member? Friend or acquaintance?

Chapter 3 – Faith Revealed through Heartaches

This chapter illustrates faith's involvement through life's heartaches of relationship conflicts, divorce, step-parenting, single parenthood and death.

- How does faith relate to relational issues such as divorce and step-parenting?
- Discuss the challenges of faith during times of sudden relational loss like infidelity of a spouse, accidental death of a spouse or family member, and divorce.
- Discuss the church's position on divorce and re-marriage for clergy. Do you agree or disagree with those church positions?

Chapter 4 – Faith Revealed through Wilderness Experiences

This chapter addresses those times in our life when we feel overrun by wild circumstances that were neither planned nor ever expected to be encountered. The author characterizes these experiences as when suddenly what we know to be, no longer bears any resemblance to anything we knew before, not sure how things changed so dramatically and with no idea how to get out of the new circumstance.

- Discuss any wilderness experiences in the group.
- Discuss the importance of faith during a wilderness experience.
- The author's account during his wilderness experience describes himself as being consumed with physical, financial, and emotional worries, no longer thinking about spiritual things and feeling as though all connection to God was lost. What would be your approach to help someone in that condition?

Chapter 5 – Consequences of Faith

In this chapter the author describes the "consequences of our faith" as simply the outcomes of our faith fostered and shaped by our respective communities of faith. The author further suggests that these consequences of faith can be different in the various evangelical communities and illustrates that point through his own experiences in different denominations of the evangelical church.

- Discuss the consequences of faith experienced in the group. Do you agree with the author's observation of different consequences for different denominations?

- The author uses Hebrews 12:29 "For God is a consuming fire" as a scriptural illustration of the consequences of faith. Do you agree or disagree? Please explain.
- The author suggests that God is not the inventor of the doctrine that accommodates the peculiarities of our particular community of faith. He further states that doctrines are man's interpretation of God's intent. Do you agree or disagree? Please explain.

Chapter 6 – Evolution of Faith

This chapter suggests that there is a natural maturing to our faith, or progression if you will, in all our faith experiences. The author suggests Romans 1:17 validates this principle as it states - "For in it (referring to the gospel of Christ) the righteousness of God is revealed from faith to faith." The author contends that faith is not only continuous, but also it is a sequence of events on that continuum of time.

- Do you believe our faith evolves? Please explain why or why not.
- The author suggests that our faith's evolution often occurs through incremental steps described as events, epiphanies, or revelations. Please describe any such events that you may have experienced that increased your faith.
- The author suggests the evolution of our faith increases the intimacy of our relationship with God. Do you agree or disagree? Please explain.

Chapter 7 – Certainties of Faith

In this chapter the author suggests that there are two certainties of faith: God exists, and He rewards those who seek Him (Hebrews

11:6). The author also suggests that as faith grows, perspectives of our faith begin to change. Finally, the author suggests that denominational differences can be attributed in part to an emphasis on dogma (principles or beliefs put forth as authoritative without adequate grounds) rather than doctrine (the body of principles or positions of a particular system of belief).

- What are your certainties of faith?
- Have you had the experience of your faith's perspective changing over time? If so, in what way?
- Do you agree with the author's suggestion of the causes in denominational differences being from belief in doctrine versus dogma? Please explain why or why not.

Chapter 8 – Integrity of Faith

In this chapter the author suggests our faith should demonstrate a consistency in our actions, motives, intentions, and spirit that conform to our beliefs. Any division between our faith (what we believe) and our motives or attitudes and our actions would be a lack of integrity among these elements.

- Do you agree with the author's position on integrity of faith? Please explain.
- The author states that any intentional conduct in direct violation of federal, state, or local law should not be embraced because of the violation of scriptural principal of being subject to our authorities (Romans 13:1-3, 1 Peter 2:13-14). Do you agree or disagree? Do you believe there are exceptions to the rule? Please explain.

Chapter 9 – One Nation Under God

This chapter discusses the concept of being "one nation under God" as stated in our pledge of allegiance to our flag. The author suggests that we cannot be "one nation under God" until the communities of faith accept other faiths and address racism in the church.

- The author suggests that accepting other faiths doesn't mean all faiths have to be the same but should respect and be in fellowship with one another to represent one nation under God. Do you agree with this concept? Why or why not?
- The author suggests addressing racism in faith communities will require that those both white and those of color, begin "to see" each other. This means that both types of faith communities must move on from the superficial relationships that predominately exist to a more meaningful understanding of issues on both sides of racism. Please discuss any experiences you have had in your faith communities trying to solve racism. Do you agree with the authors position? Why or why not?

Chapter 10 – The Polarization of Faith

This chapter discusses the "polarization" of faith communities which is defined as to be divided into two distinct groups with no middle ground. The author contends that this polarization often causes "single issue" voting which results in supporting political candidates that demonstrate very little "integrity of faith" as discussed in Chapter 8.

- Do you agree or disagree with this characterization of evangelical "single issue" voting in political elections? Please explain.

- The author describes that his "single issue" was abortion and that it constrained his political allegiances for many years. Do you agree or disagree with the author's view that changing from being a "single issue" voter over abortion rights enables a more objective view when voting for a political candidate? Please explain.
- Do you agree that laws that represent moral decisions (like abortion/drunk driving) are not equitable if the science that governs the law (i.e., definition the begin/end of life) is not as precise in the measuring of the outcome of violating the law (i.e., level of blood alcohol to determine drunk driving)? Please explain why or why not.
- When does life begin in your opinion and what is the basis? Please identify any scriptural references if used as a basis.
- Is it ever justified to end a life prematurely? When is it justified to remove someone from life support? What is the basis for these answers and identify any scriptural references if used.

Chapter 11 – Electing the Elect

This chapter suggests that the communities of faith, scripturally identified as "the elect" should select leaders of our country that model the values held in high regard in faith communities such as truth, grace, patience, and kindness.

- Do you agree with the author's position that the faith community should expect and demand our leaders to lead with integrity, honesty, compassion and most of all with the greater good in mind?
- In your experience, what approximate percentage would you estimate of your elected officials (local, state, and Federal levels) represent these values: 25%, 50%, 75% or

100%? Please explain why. Are you satisfied with the % represented?

- Over the last 10 presidents what percentage would you estimate represent these values? (0 – 100%) Please explain why. Are you satisfied with the % represented? (Note last 10 presidents: Biden, Trump, Obama, Bush G.W., Clinton, Bush G., Reagan, Carter, Ford, Nixon)

Chapter 12 – Faith and the Constitution

This chapter discusses the irony that although freedom of religion is a cornerstone of our constitution, that free exercise has led to abhorrent behaviors in our country starting from before the Civil War to our present-day experiences. The author suggests that the confluence of religion and politics or faith and governance is a complex problem for our nation.

- Do you think of our nation as being a Christian nation or at least it should be considered a Christian nation? Why or why not?
- The author states that a blend of faith and political will has been nurtured in our nation over the last few years culminating on Jan.6, 2021 when a political rally turned into an assault on Capitol Hill. Do you agree with this assessment? Why or why not?
- The author states that if our faith has directly or indirectly made us complicit in a crisis that causes the destruction of our democracy, protected by the same constitution that protects our freedom of religion, then we have truly lost our way as a nation and a people of faith. Do you agree with that statement? Why or why not?

- Do you agree with the authors position on the 2nd amendment and the prohibition of automatic weapons? Why or why not?

Chapter 13 – Pew versus Platform

This chapter starts the final part of the book that suggests how to move away from an emphasis on learning about faith and allows a time and opportunity to experience faith.

- The author suggests that the typical church experience has become platform-centric, constrained in time, with tightly controlled agendas because of multiple services, leaving little opportunity to "experience" God. Do you agree with this assessment? Why or why not?
- The author suggests that services that afford an opportunity to "experience" God are those that touch hearts, heals souls, and builds faith. The author further suggests that these experiences do not happen quickly, they must be nurtured and not rushed. Have you ever been part of a similar gathering? If so, describe the environment and the outcomes.
- The author suggests that the problems in our nation are physical outcomes as a result of spiritual influences dictated by our faith. He further suggests our faith experiences dictate the attitude of our hearts and minds. Do you agree or disagree with the author's position? Please explain.

Chapter 14 – Such a Time as This

This chapter continues to suggest how to move away from an emphasis on learning about faith and allowing a time and opportunity to experience faith.

- The author suggests we are in a time in which communities of faith are experiencing an *identity crisis* which occurs when an erosion of core values has such an effect on the outcomes of our faith that we are without distinction from people without faith. Do you agree with this position? Why or why not?
- The author suggests the evangelical communities of faith are in a season in which change is required away from theological debate to a statement made through action. The evidence of this is the general state of the evangelical church today: more have left the church then remain in it; most evangelicals go occasionally and casually without purpose or passion; and most of the work is done by a few. Do you agree with this position? Why or why not?

Chapter 15 – Different Methods for Different Outcomes

The book concludes with this final chapter with a discussion on how to move away from an emphasis on learning about faith and allowing a time and opportunity to experience faith.

- The author suggests that what is needed now is a new dimension to come alongside of our existing faith communities in which one can attend in anticipation of having an experience with God. Do you agree with this concept? Would you be open to attend such a gathering? Why or why not?
- The author proposes a network of informal gatherings where the focus would be on worship, prayer for one another and being open to experiencing the presence of God. Would you be interested in participating in such an experience? Why or why not?

ENDNOTE

Part of the vision for this writing was to spark an interest in the people of faith to meet with the hope of a fresh experience with the God of their faith. The approach would consist of informal gatherings in designated places where the focus would be on worship, prayer for one another, and being open to experiencing the presence of God. What I propose is a network only associated by its approach to the faith experience that informally communicates through social media of a general listing of gatherings when and where they occur. The website **faithforthetimes.net** has been launched to act as a conduit to facilitate such gatherings. If you have any interest in facilitating, organizing, or attending such a gathering refer to this site for the latest information. Let's gather together "for such a time as this".

ABOUT THE AUTHOR

Born in Philadelphia, Pa. I spent my youth in Flemington, New Jersey the home of the Lindbergh baby-kidnapping trial and the once famous Flemington Cut Glass that is no longer there. I spent most of my adult life in the northern Virginia area, except for my college years in Lexington and a few years living on the eastern shore on Chincoteague Island. I am now retired with my wife, living in the Annapolis, Maryland area.

My faith journey is unique in both its scope and its intensity. Starting as a Catholic child and almost being recruited into the priesthood, my faith took an extreme turn as an adult into various evangelical communities beginning as an Independent Baptist and concluding as an ordained minister in the Pentecostal Holiness Church. Included in this text are my experiences in the Assembly of God and independent Pentecostal churches including starting my own independent Pentecostal church until it was merged as part of the Pentecostal Holiness Church denomination. My sacred experiences include teaching, counseling, ministering, and pastoring. These blend with my secular experiences of teaching in the public-school system for five years and a 30-year career of civil service in the Federal Government. My public high school teaching experience of approximately seven years included four different school systems in two different states and covered a variety of classes in Algebra, Geometry and Trigonometry. My civil service career included positions in several agencies within the Departments of Defense and Transportation. Assignments were in engineering and program management culminating with a temporary senior executive appointment for six months. This broad range of experiences resulted in a unique view of how faith is realized and its influence on the political outcomes of our nation.

The urgency of this publication is in its relevance to our current times with regard to how people of faith vote, how they react to political events, and ultimately how they view the function of our government including the interpretation of our constitution. I believe this view was fostered spending many years working in the halls of our federal government by day and ministering in the D.C. area in my spare time, nights, and weekends. I believe this book contains a unique message that is relevant for this unique time in our nation. I hope it is of value to all who take the time to read it.

Printed in the United States
by Baker & Taylor Publisher Services